Healed
FROM A BENT
Condition

THELMA GILBERT, M.A., D.D.

WESTBOW
PRESS®
A DIVISION OF THOMAS NELSON
& ZONDERVAN

Author Photo by Chantrail Maybelle Simmons
Front Cover Photo by Kenric Austin Prescott, M.S.W.,
M.Div. http://kapturedphotos.redbubble.com

WestBow Press books may be ordered through booksellers or by contacting:

WestBow Press
A Division of Thomas Nelson & Zondervan
1663 Liberty Drive
Bloomington, IN 47403
www.westbowpress.com
1 (866) 928-1240

ISBN: 978-1-5127-2488-2 (sc)
ISBN: 978-1-5127-2490-5 (hc)
ISBN: 978-1-5127-2489-9 (e)

Library of Congress Control Number: 2015921201

Print information available on the last page.

WestBow Press rev. date: 1/8/2016

Contents

In loving memory of three people I miss dearly: my mother, the late Osceola Simmons, and my two sisters, the late Marjorie Gibson and the late Maybelle Simmons

Comments about the Author

Rev. Dr. Thelma Gilbert is a woman after the heart of God. God hath spoken concerning you: "Greater!" Oh, taste and see that the Lord is blessing your journey as you travel down Destiny Road! Press on!

—Presiding Bishop Jean B. Taylor
Jehovah-Jireh Ministries International

It is a genuine honor to count Rev. Dr. Thelma Gilbert a dear friend. She is an anointed and committed servant of God. She is a great organizer and administrator. Rev. Gilbert is quite humble and always is committed to helping others. Her book *Healed from a Bent Condition* is both inspiring and encouraging. It is destined to touch with meaningful impact all who shall read its pages.

—Vincent L. Thompson Jr., MSW, M.Div., D.Min.
Pastor and Teacher

Rev. Dr. Gilbert has availed herself to be the canvas for God's works. She has made her life one of learning, teaching, loving, giving, receiving, administering, falling, recovering, and always standing on faith. The reader will get a glimpse of her journey in progress through these pages.

—Tanya Johnson-Gilchrist, LCSW, MPH, CPH

The Rev. Dr. Thelma Gilbert is truly a woman of God. Dr. Gilbert has been called a trailblazer for women. She has paved the way for women of all ages, nationalities, and faiths in ministry. She is indeed a woman with great talents given to her by God. Over the years, she has unselfishly given of herself to others by serving God and humanity.

—Minister Tina Williams-Knight

Pastor Thelma Gilbert, (Mama T), as I call her, is a remarkable, anointed, persevering, gift to the body of Christ.

Her infectious smile, intelligence, graciousness in giving to others, flows out of a reservoir of the grace God has entrusted to her. Rev. Dr. Thelma Gilbert, the first female President of the Greater Hartford Interdenominational Ministerial Alliance, is a trail blazer, a spiritual mentor and teacher to women pastors, ministers, and laymen, in the state of Connecticut.

--Lydia P. Ford
Pastor of "Don't Forget To Say Your Prayers Ministry"

Thelma and I have been friends for over forty years. I watched Thelma grow from a person of low self esteem to the strong woman she is today. I could compare her transformation in life to the metamorphosis of the butterfly. Her faith in God, through all of her trials, never waivered.

--Dorothy L Googe

Foreword

THE AUTHOR, DR. THELMA GILBERT, and I have much in common. At some point in our lives, we've personally experienced illness or watched loved ones suffer through diseases, disabilities, and deaths due to relentless maladies. Maladies affect all sizes, races, and cultures. Maladies have no regard for our spiritual or religious backgrounds. When disorders assault our lives, questions naturally arise. We ask, "Why me? Is there no end to my suffering? How did this suffering find me?" Our experiences seem to parallel those of the apostle Paul, and we wonder if Satan sent the suffering to taunt, buffet, and defeat us (2 Corinthians 12:7). Are our disabilities and diseases the results of our personal sins or those of our parents (John 9:1–2)? Does illness come as a test initiated by Satan but sanctioned by the Lord (Job 2:1–7)? On the other hand, are the woes in our lives sent to give glory to God, as John 11:4 suggests?

Some sicknesses are short-lived, while others abide throughout our lives. When they settle in for the long run, we need a strategy to contest them and claim victory over them. In *Healed from a Bent Condition*, Dr. Gilbert unveils her personal path from a bent condition to relief and healing.

I have known Dr. Gilbert for nineteen years and have found her to be an insightful and able preacher, teacher, church planter, and retreat facilitator. I knew of her tenderhearted work as a human services professional and her call to ministry and the pastorate, yet only as I read her book did I learn that she is one of the wounded healers Henri Nouwen describes in his book *The Wounded Healer*.

Thelma describes the personal wounds that almost devastated her. She speaks of personal demons that tested her faith that left her desperate, depressed and devastated. As with Job,[1] she wondered about the presence of God in the midst of her suffering. She describes a five-year battle for her life as she accepted her doctor's prescriptions for psychotropic meds. Thelma describes her addiction to prescribed medications that put her in a zombielike state. She identifies herself with the biblical account of a woman with a bent-over condition (Luke 13:10–17), and with gut-wrenching truth, she confesses her prayers for miracles. She saw no miracle, yet her faith did not fail.

There were times when she conducted Freudian self-analysis, trying to learn the formula for her own healing. In this book, she weaves her life story with biblically grounded and theologically sound reasoning. In time, she got to a place where she discovered the essence of Nouwen's message:

---

[1] Job 23:3.

"The beginning and the end of all Christian leadership is to give your life for others."[2]

I was honored by her request to write the foreword for her book. Regrettably, I have only known her since her release from her bent-over condition. I wish I had known her before her transformation. In fact, whenever you read gospel accounts of people who received relief from their maladies, in most cases, you'll discover that the healed, exorcized, or resurrected people received whole and malady-free lives.

In a few gospel accounts, we see people celebrating their unbent conditions. Some leaped (Acts 14:9–1), some returned home (Matthew 9:8), and the woman who was cured after twelve years of bleeding (Matthew 9:22) simply slipped into the crowd and was never seen again. However, I love the accounts in which people's healings, exorcisms, restorations, and resurrections end up with people celebrating and telling everyone the good news (Matthew 8:2–3, 9:27–31; Mark 5:18–20; Luke 7:11–18).

With this book, Thelma testifies of her faith in the life, death, and resurrection of Jesus Christ. She celebrates the transformation the Lord performed in her life, and as with others in the Bible, she has been testifying of the great things the Lord has done for her. Because of the Lord's goodness and grace, she has poured out her life in service to God and humanity. She has given herself over to the work of bringing help, healing, and hope to others.

---

[2] Henri J. M. Nouwen, *The Wounded Healer: Ministry in Contemporary Society*, accessed July 23, 2015, http://www.goodreads.com/work/quotes/1202823-the-wounded-healer.

Since overcoming her bent-over condition, she has engaged in pastoral and human service work that has opened new vistas and opportunities for many. Her unbent state of life has resulted in ministries rendered to the glory and honor of the Lord.

Kenric A. Prescott
Pastor and Teacher, Union Baptist
Church of Hartford, Connecticut

Preface

WHEN I STARTED TO WRITE this book, I intended to write a book of sermons. During that time in my life, I was going through a wilderness experience with God. I was waiting for the Holy Spirit to direct my next steps in ministry. To my amazement, as I started writing the first sermon on the miracle of the woman with the spirit of infirmity, the Holy Spirit guided my thoughts in a direction I never could have imagined. Surprisingly, this story, located in Luke 13:10–17, started developing into a book of its own. It was then that I realized my next step was to write this book. This twist confounded my spirit and mind. I tossed my plans for the book of sermons out the window, remembering what my mother used to say to me: "We plan, but God unplans." How true this statement has been concerning this book and my life as a whole. My mother experienced and understood what Jeremiah 29:11 meant far better than I did. I encourage you to accept the truth of God's Word, as I did, as you read the following verse of Scripture: "For I know the plans I have for you,' declares the LORD, 'plans to prosper you

and not to harm you, plans to give you hope and a future"
(NIV).

I thank God for my mother's wisdom, but most of all, I thank God for knowing the plans He has for my life. The wisdom and insight I received from the ministry of the Holy Spirit while writing this book were miracles in and of themselves. I am eternally grateful to God for entrusting me with this challenging task.

In the miracle of the woman described in Luke 13:10–17, there are four different players. The first is a woman who has a disability called "a spirit of infirmity"; the second is Christ, the healer; the third is a faultfinding ruler; and the fourth is a grateful crowd. When you read of this supernatural act performed by Jesus Christ, I pray the working ministry of the Holy Spirit will deepen your understanding of His Word and enlighten you with new revelations from His heavenly throne. Hopefully you will come to the realization that every human being, in one way or another, is crippled with a spirit of infirmity. While you read this book, I hope you will gain a keen awareness of the fact that we need a healing Christ in our lives, individually and collectively.

It is my desire that when you receive your healing from Jesus, the Great Physician, you will share your testimony with others. While sharing your testimony and rejoicing in the Lord, give God all the glory. Let your testimony be so convincing and powerful that others will know that

> God can do anything, you know—far more
> than you could ever imagine or guess or

request in your wildest dreams! He does it not by pushing us around but by working within us, his Spirit deeply and gently within us. (Ephesians 3:20 MSG)

While you continue growing in the grace and knowledge of Jesus Christ, I pray that your faith in God will increase, your trust in Him will deepen, and your hope in His miraculous power will become secure. As you travel your Christian journey, I hope you will know how to discern who is for you and who is against you. Just as there were faultfinding and trap-laying people who entered the synagogue with the wrong motives during Jesus's earthly ministry, faultfinding and trap-laying people exist in the body of Christ today. Some attend our church services and Bible study sessions with wrong motives in their minds. Because we decided to serve the Lord, we are their targets. Their main purpose is to seek and destroy whomever they may devour. On the other hand, there are dedicated and loving people who desire to serve the Lord with all their hearts. They will celebrate and praise God with you for your healing. Although you do not understand the whys of the Holy Spirit and His leadings, remember what God said in Isaiah 55:8–9:

> "For my thoughts are not your thoughts, neither are your ways my ways," declares the LORD. "As the heavens are higher than the earth, so are my ways higher than your ways and my thoughts than your thoughts." (NIV)

Some researchers say Jesus performed approximately thirty-five to forty miracles during His earthly ministry. The blind miraculously received their sight (John 9:1–7). The deaf could hear, and the dumb could speak (Matthew 9:32). The sick and diseased were made whole (Luke 5:12–15). People who were possessed with demons were restored to their right minds and spiritual insight (Mark 1:23–28). Multitudes were fed with only seven loaves of bread and a few small fish (Mark 8:1–10). Jesus walked on water (John 6:15–21), raised the dead, and restored a woman's health (Luke 8:40–56). Jesus performed many other miracles during His earthly ministry that are not recorded in the Bible. John tells us,

> Jesus performed many other signs in the presence of his disciples, which are not recorded in this book. But these are written that you may believe that Jesus is the Messiah, the Son of God, and that by believing you may have life in his name. (John 20:30 NIV)

Jesus did not perform miracles for his own personal gain, pride, or self-gratification. He performed them to prove that God intervenes in the normal course of nature, events, and affairs in our lives (Joshua 10:1–15). His miracles were to prove that He is the Son of God (Matthew 14:33) and the promised Messiah (John 1:41). Jesus performed miracles so that people would believe in His name (John 6:29) and to strengthen their faith in Him (Luke 8:46) and show compassion for humanity (Mark 6:34).

As you read this book, you will discover that I use the terms *spirit of infirmity, bent-over condition,* and *disability* interchangeably as a frame of reference. There are also times when I couple the sayings.

It is my prayer that this book will be a blessing to you.

To God be the glory!

Acknowledgments

First and foremost, I give all praises and honor to God for empowering me with the wisdom and knowledge to write this book. Without His guidance and power, I could not have accomplished this divine assignment. I am reminded of what Philippians 4:13 says: "I can do all things through Christ which strengtheneth me." All glory and blessings go to God for the successful completion of this book.

I would like to express my deep and sincere gratitude to my pastor, Kenric A. Prescott, pastor and teacher at Union Baptist Church of Hartford, for traveling along this journey with me. I am thankful for your invaluable knowledge, faithfulness, input, guidance, love, proofreading, and patience with me throughout this process. I also thank you for your pastoral leadership, friendship, empathy, and sense of humor.

I am also grateful to Pastor Prescott's wife, Elder Deborah Prescott, for her encouragement, sisterhood, and love through this process. I am truly grateful for your deep commitment and dedication to the Lord.

I am extremely indebted to my mother, the late Osceola Simmons, for her motherly love, prayers, and guidance and for all of her sacrifices in educating me and preparing me for my future. I am thankful for my late sister Maybelle Simmons input and comments about this book before her passing. I am beholden to my only living sibling, Marcus Simmons, for his love, constant encouragement, and input concerning this work. I love him dearly. To my niece, Tanya Johnson, thank you for your love, insight, excitement, and continual support. Your encouragement has meant a lot to me.

I would like to thank my colleagues Reverend Dr. Vincent Thompson, Reverend Dr. Joshua McClure, Reverend Asalene Brown, Elder Sonya Green, and Minister Tina Willams-Knight, my spiritual daughters in ministry, for their love, support, input, and comments concerning this work.

Finally, I extend my gratitude to all the people who prayed for me and supported me in one way or another as I was completing *Healed from a Bent Condition*.

God bless each and every one of you.

Scripture

ON A SABBATH JESUS WAS teaching in one of the synagogues, and a woman was there who had been crippled by a spirit for eighteen years. She was bent over and could not straighten up at all. When Jesus saw her, he called her forward and said to her, "Woman, you are set free from your infirmity." Then he put his hands on her, and immediately she straightened up and praised God. Indignant because Jesus had healed on the Sabbath, the synagogue ruler said to the people, "There are six days for work. So come and be healed on those days, not on the Sabbath." The Lord answered him, "You hypocrites! Doesn't each of you on the Sabbath untie his ox or donkey from the stall and lead it out to give it water? Then should not this woman, a daughter of Abraham, whom Satan has kept bound for eighteen long years be set free on the Sabbath day from what bound her?" When he said this, all his opponents were humiliated, but the people were delighted with all the wonderful things he was doing. (Luke 13:10–17 NIV)

Childhood and Adolescence

WHEN I WAS GROWING UP, I attended a Catholic school. One of our daily subjects was catechism. During class, we had to read and discuss the Bible, and we received homework assignments. The subject that excited me most was the miracles of the Bible, especially the ones Jesus performed.

To me, there was just something special about this man named Jesus. When I read the Bible, I believed what it said about His miracles. In studying how He turned water into wine (John 2:1–11), calmed a raging sea (Mark 4:35–41), fed five thousand people with five loaves of bread and two fish (Mark 6:30–44), healed a deaf mute (Mark 7:31–37), and restored sight to the blind (Mark 8:22–26), I believe God's Word. I accepted the fact that "with God nothing shall be impossible" (Luke 1:37).

Reading about the miracles Jesus preformed made me feel as if I were right there on the scene as the miraculous events were happening. When I shared with others what seemed real to me, some of them said, "Oh, you were just fantasizing." For me, though, the miracle stories written about Jesus in the four Gospels came alive in my spirit.

They were real events to me. I did not want to hear anyone say I was fantasizing, because I felt that meant they were denying that Jesus could do anything but fail.

I believed then, as I believe now, that Jesus Christ could perform any miracle. It didn't matter how unbelievable the narratives sounded to other people or how impossible it seemed for others to accept the stories as true. The miracles were true to me. Why? Because of who Jesus is. He is omniscient (Hebrews 4:13), omnipotent (Jeremiah 32:17), omnipresent (Psalm 139:7–12), and immutable (Malachi 3:6). He is from everlasting to everlasting (Psalm 41:13). He is one with the Father (John 17:22). He is God all by Himself, and besides Him, there is no other (Isaiah 45:5). Since God said it, I believed it, and that settled it.

That was the kind of faith I had in Jesus as a child. If nothing is impossible for God, then whatever is impossible for man is fully possible with God. He can take nothing and create something. Whatever is crooked, He can make straight. Whatever is broken, He can make whole. Whatever is cast out, He can take in. Whatever is knocked down, He can pick up. Whatever is way down in the valley, He can put on a mountaintop. God is sovereign. He is the almighty God. He is the great I Am. Think about it: if He could call chaos into order and create something out of nothing just by saying, "Let there be" (Genesis 1:3), it is evident He can do anything—even the impossible.

My Request and the Issue of Judging

DURING MY CHILDHOOD AND ADOLESCENCE, my faith was strong in the Master Healer. All I desired from God, from the depths of my soul, was for Him to perform what I called a radical, supernatural miracle in my life. I knew He woke me up in the morning and started me on my way, but I was seeking and talking about something deeper than that. I wanted to experience Jesus in the spiritual realm. I wanted to taste heaven down here on Earth, even though I did not understand what that really meant.

During the first eight years of school, I had to attend Mass almost every day. While sitting in the midst of the congregation during the service, I would be waiting for something extraordinary to happen to me. If it didn't happen by the time we were in the middle of the service, I would ask Jesus (quietly, that is) to lift me out of my seat and suspend me in the air. I even had the nerve to ask Him to put a bright halo around my head so that others would believe He was real. During those years, I felt that many of my classmates didn't believe that Jesus could perform miraculous acts or that He was as real as I believed.

When reflecting back on that time in my life, I have to ask myself, *Who was I to judge someone else's faith in God?* I had some nerve during those early years of my life. Back then, I didn't know I was judging other people's faith, nor did I give any thought to my behavior. I wasn't thinking about what the Bible says in Matthew 7:1–2 and James 3:1–2 about judging others, because my mind was too busy seeking the miraculous. Now when I read the following Scriptures, they remind me of how warped my attitude was about judging others:

> Do not judge, or you too will be judged. For in the same way you judge others, you will be judged, and with the measure you use, it will be measured to you. (Matthew 7:1–2 NIV)
> Not many of you should become teachers, my fellow believers, because you know that we who teach will be judged more strictly. We all stumble in many ways. Anyone who is never at fault in what they say is perfect, able to keep their whole body in check. (James 3:1–2 NIV)

Although catechism was one of my daily subjects, I did not fully understand what I was studying. I was a child, not an adult, and I used that as an excuse for my ignorance. Now that I am an adult and a maturing Christian continuously growing in the grace and knowledge of Jesus Christ, I can no longer use being a child as an excuse. I now realize those Scriptures are powerful and profound.

As a child, I failed miserably in the way I thought about people's faith in God. As an adult, I still find myself judging other people's faith, actions, and thoughts about life and have to ask God if I am judging a particular situation or discerning something I need to see or learn. I need to know the difference so that I can work on my criticism of others, even if I'm criticizing them only in my mind. There is a saying that you can't judge a book by its cover. You have to read the book to find out what it is about.

I am still in the process of becoming all that Jesus wants me to become in Him, which means I need the Holy Spirit to work on me every day of my life. The apostle Paul tells us in Romans 14:10–13,

> You, then, why do you judge your brother or sister? Or why do you treat them with contempt? For we will all stand before God's judgment seat. It is written: "As surely as I live," says the Lord, "every knee will bow before me; every tongue will acknowledge God." So then, each of us will give an account of ourselves to God. Therefore let us stop passing judgment on one another. Instead, make up your mind not to put any stumbling block or obstacle in the way of a brother or sister. (NIV)

I thank God for forgiving my sins and working with me on the issue of judging others and on all of my other shortcomings. One day all of us will have to give an account before God for our actions, words, thoughts, and deeds, including all of our sins and shortcomings.

Judgmental, Critical, and Faultfinding Spirits

AFTER READING MATTHEW 7:1–2 AND James 3:1–2, my spirit was enlightened to a deeper understanding about judging others.

Three types of spirits came to mind that ruin relationships and cause a great deal of dissension among the people of God: a judgmental spirit, a critical spirit, and a faultfinding spirit. A judgmental[3] spirit is someone who is inclined to make judgments, especially moral or personal ones, about someone else. A critical[4] spirit is someone who expresses disapproval by pointing out the faults or shortcomings of others. A faultfinding[5] spirit is someone who engages in petty or nagging criticism and tends to make judgments based on personal opinions.

---

[3] *The Free Dictionary*, s.v. "judgmental," accessed July 16, 2015, http://www.thefreedictionary.com/judgmental.

[4] *The Free Dictionary*, s.v. "criticism," accessed July 16, 2015, http://www.thefreedictionary.com/criticism.

[5] *The Free Dictionary*, s.v. "faultfinding," accessed July 16, 2015, http:/www./thefreedictionary.com/faultfinding.

We are admonished in the gospel of Matthew not to judge others, for when we judge others, we will also be judged. When we sit on the judgment seat, we give the Devil a tool to use in playing with our minds. He has many powerful ways to influence our minds about judging people. He uses judgmental spirits, critical spirits, and faultfinding spirits to destroy relationships between friends, team members, ministries, family members, and colleagues. The Word of God tells us in Philippians 2:5, "Let this mind be in you, which was also in Christ Jesus" (KJV). When we say phrases like "I think" or "I'm not sure, but" without facts, we give the Devil an open door and a tool to use in exploiting our minds.

If you think about your own life and are honest with yourself, you will acknowledge that you have judged other people's actions, behaviors, attitudes, circumstances, and faith in God. Maybe you can think of a situation in which you judged a person's motives or actions. I hope reflecting on your judgmental behavior of someone, led you to repent for that sin, as it did me. Judging others and what they were or are doing takes the focus off of your own faults, actions, behaviors, attitudes, circumstances, and faith in God and keeps you from coping with your own issues. Jesus cautions and reproves us about judging others in Matthew 7:3–5. He tells us,

> Why do you look at the speck of sawdust in your brother's eye and pay no attention to the plank in your own eye? How can you say to your brother, "Let me take the speck out of

your eye," when all the time there is a plank in your own eye? You hypocrite, first take the plank out of your own eye, and then you will see clearly to remove the speck from your brother's eye. (NIV)

Because we often can't see the planks in our own eyes, you and I need the presence and power of the Holy Spirit to point out our faults to us. We need the Holy Spirit to aid us in setting our house in order before we even think about finding fault with our fellow man. We need the Holy Spirit to reveal to us that our judgmental attitude has caused many people a great deal of torment, hardship, and pain.

As Christians, our assignment is to love our neighbors as ourselves and not chase them away from us because of opinionated and judgmental attitudes. I am sure if people knew I was judging their faith in Jesus Christ during those early years in my life, they wouldn't have wanted to associate themselves with a person who had a faultfinding or judgmental spirit. There are people living in our society today who choose to exclude themselves from being around certain people in their lives because of their judgmental attitudes and criticizing spirits.

I have been in the midst of people who judged and criticized everything and everybody. Sometimes I became involved in the process of judging others with them. For example, some people are quick to judge a homeless person without knowing why or how that individual became homeless. They are quick to call the person a bum or say the individual is lazy and doesn't want to work for a living.

When a person suffers with a serious illness, such as the woman with a spirit of infirmity, or bent-over condition, recorded in Luke 13:10–17, there might be people in that person's congregation or neighborhood who cast judgment upon him or her. For example, in the case of the woman with the spirit of infirmity, they might have said, openly or quietly within their own spirits, "I think she is reaping what she has sown," without knowing why she had been living with that type of burden for eighteen years. The ruler in Luke 13:14 criticized and judged Jesus for healing on the Sabbath Day. The Word of God says, "Indignant because Jesus had healed on the Sabbath, the synagogue leader said to the people, 'There are six days for work. So come and be healed on those days, not on the Sabbath'" (NIV).

It is important for you to understand that people will criticize you even if you don't give them anything to criticize. Some people will find fault about what you are wearing. They will judge your actions without knowing what kind of directions your supervisor gave you to carry out a particular assignment. Some people will judge your attitude and your living environment. They will criticize the way you talk, walk, and eat. They will criticize the way you pray, dress, preach, teach, sing, and even cook. Some people will always find fault about anything and everything.

It seems as if it is sometimes easier for people to focus on another person's faults, problems, or issues so that they don't have to cope with their own personal issues, shortcomings, and insecurities. My former pastor, who is now deceased, used to say, "I have six months to mind my own business and another six months to leave everybody else's alone." If we live with this kind of attitude, we will not have time to exercise a judgmental spirit or a spirit of criticism or faultfinding. We need to realize that when we criticize other people, we are not giving God glory. Instead, we are giving our opinion, which oftentimes leads to judging others and glorifying the works of the Devil and not God.

Until now, I have never openly stated that I used to judge other people's faith in God, especially when I was in the sixth through eighth grades. When I did so, I was sinning against God in my mind and spirit, because inwardly, I was judging and criticizing other people's faith. As I think about my old mind-set now, I realize I was frowning upon what I thought others were believing, feeling and thinking. Without realizing it, I was devaluing their faith, intelligence, and integrity, as well as thinking of them as less than I was. I repented for my sin and asked Jesus to forgive me not just for judging other people's faith in Him but also for judging people period. I am amazed how God uses imperfect people to carry out His perfect will in order to build up His kingdom. What a forgiving God we serve. I have learned through the years that no human being in this world, no matter how long he or she lives, will ever understand God's ways. His ways and thoughts are not our ways and thoughts. They are beyond our ability to find out. Neither will we ever fully understand the Word of God. In spite of this, the Word of God is true, though it is mysterious.

We all have judged, criticized, and found fault with other people during the course of our lifetimes. We have done it knowingly or unknowingly. We must realize that no one has the right to find fault with or disapprove of another individual's actions or behaviors and place his or her personal sentence upon that person. When we judge others, we are acting as if we are God, sitting on a throne. God is the judge of every man, not us. Romans 12:3 tells us,

> For by the grace given me I say to every one of you: Do not think of yourself more highly than you ought, but rather think of yourself with sober judgment, in accordance with the measure of faith God has given you. (NIV)

We should never think of ourselves as too high-minded or have too high an opinion of ourselves. When we think this way, we give the Devil room to play with our minds. The apostle Paul tells us in Romans 12:2, "And do not be conformed to this world, but be transformed by the renewing of your mind, that you may prove what is that good and acceptable and perfect will of God" (NIV).

Not So Special

SEVERAL QUESTIONS REMAIN: WHO WAS I? Why did I think I was so special that Jesus, the God-man, who came down through forty-two generations, would perform this miraculous event through me and for me and not through or for someone else? Who was I to make such a request? I was an ordinary, imperfect person just like everyone else in the assembly. We all needed Jesus to save us by His redeeming grace and perform miracles in our lives.

Well, evidently I was not as special as I thought, because neither one of those radical supernatural encounters happened to me during my twelve years in school. I didn't even think I was special; I just wanted Jesus to perform a miracle in my life because I knew He could. I can't explain or articulate to you how I knew, besides His Word saying so. In fact, His Word was all I needed in order to believe He could do anything but fail. I did not lose my faith in Jesus Christ because He didn't grant me my request. I kept believing by faith that He could do the impossible in a person's life when He deemed it necessary.

By now, you might be thinking that I was foolish in the way I thought as a child and that my faith in Jesus Christ was perhaps somewhat unrealistic. You have my permission to think that way. I don't mind at all, because what I believed as a child helped me to become a stronger believer in Jesus Christ today. The funny thing about my begging for a miracle is that I did not understand the explanation or definition of the word *miracle*. All I knew during those years was that no matter how impossible Jesus's miracles sounded in the stories, He could turn an impossible situation into a possible one. Although I lacked knowledge about the definition and meaning of a miracle, I believed as a child—and I still believe—the miracles of Jesus are just as real today as they were then; in fact, I believe it even more so now as I continue growing in God's grace and in my faith in Jesus Christ.

If you need a miracle in your life today, I have good news for you: God is still working miracles in the lives of His people every day. How He performs these miracles remains a mystery to me today, just as it was for people in biblical times. This might sound foolish to you, but it does not sound foolish to me. I believe the words of the apostle Paul in 1 Corinthians 1:25, 27–31:

> For the foolishness of God is wiser than human wisdom, and the weakness of God is stronger than human strength ... But God chose the foolish things of the world to shame the wise; God chose the weak things of the world to shame the strong. God chose the lowly things

of this world and the despised things—and the things that are not—to nullify the things that are, so that no one may boast before him. It is because of him that you are in Christ Jesus, who has become for us wisdom from God—that is, our righteousness, holiness and redemption. Therefore, as it is written: "Let the one who boasts boast in the Lord." (NIV)

What Would I Have Done?

IF SOMETHING MIRACULOUS HAD HAPPENED to me during those early years in my life and I had shared that experience with other people, they probably would have thought I had lost my mind. Based on how the people in my life thought and were during my childhood and teenage years, I believe they probably would have made every effort to convince my mother to commit me to a mental institution. Even at an early age, I recognized that many people demonstrated a weak faith in Jesus Christ and His resurrection from the dead, just as some people manifest a weak faith in Him and His resurrected power today. This is not a judgmental statement but a fact.

When I think about my request for a miracle now as an adult, I ask myself the following question: What would I have done if Jesus had honored my request during my childhood or teenage years? Well, I can't answer this question, because Jesus did not grant me my request. Only God, who is omniscient, meaning "all knowing," could answer this question. In fact, the more I think about my request now, the more I realize that maybe I wouldn't have praised God and given Him the glory, as the woman in Luke 13:10–17 did. She'd had a disability called "a spirit of infirmity" for eighteen long years, but it didn't stop her from praising God (Luke 13:11). It's also possible I would have boasted to others about myself and what I'd experienced and not boasted in the Lord. Maybe my praises to God would have been self-centered praises. I might have said, "Hey, everybody, look at me," instead of saying, "Look what Jesus did for me." The Word of God tells us, "Let everything that has breath praise the LORD" (Psalm 150:6 NIV) and "For it is by grace you have been saved, through faith—and this is not from yourselves, it is the gift of God—not by works, so that no one can boast" (Ephesians 2:8–9 NIV).

Yet many times, we focus our praises on me, myself and I, and not on the God of our salvation and the Great Master of miracles. We have so much for which to praise God. We are commanded to give God the praise. As you read the following verses of Scripture, meditate on the psalmist's words.

> O give thanks unto the LORD; for he is good: for his mercy endureth forever. (Psalm 136:1 KJV)
>
> I will bless the LORD at all times; His praise shall continually be in my mouth. (Psalm 34:1 NKJV)
>
> Bless the LORD, O my soul; And all that is within me, bless His holy name! Bless the

LORD, O my soul, And forget not all His benefits: Who forgives all your iniquities, Who heals all your diseases, Who redeems your life from destruction, Who crowns you with loving-kindness and tender mercies, Who satisfies your mouth with good things, So that your youth is renewed like the eagle's. (Psalm 103:1–5 NKJV)

We must always remember that God sent His Son to become a humble servant and to die in the most despicable way: on a cross (Philippians 2:6–8). He alone is the way, the truth, and the life (John 14:6). He is the one we need to boast about, because all honor, glory, and praises belong to Him.

Request Granted

To my amazement, in 1977, during a revival service, God granted my request. I experienced a supernatural encounter with Jesus Christ by the power of God under the anointing of the Holy Spirit. I will discuss this miracle in greater detail later on in the manuscript. The miracle was not only supernatural but also radical, something like the miracle I had asked for when I sat in the midst of the congregation during my school years. No, God did not lift me out of my seat and suspend me in the air, as I'd asked Him to do many years ago, nor did He put a bright halo around my head while I sat in the midst of the congregation. If He did, I wasn't aware of it, because I was caught up in the spirit realm. God had another miraculous plan for my life that was different from what I had requested of Him as a child. After all, knowing what I know now as a mature Christian who no longer drinks milk like a babe (1 Corinthians 3:2), I have grown to realize that God's ways are not our ways, and His thoughts are not our thoughts. The Word of God makes this clear for us in Isaiah 55:8–11.

"For my thoughts are not your thoughts, neither are your ways my ways," declares the LORD. "As the heavens are higher than the earth, so are my ways higher than your ways and my thoughts than your thoughts. As the rain and the snow come down from heaven, and do not return to it without watering the earth and making it bud and flourish, so that it yields seed for the sower and bread for the eater, so is my word that goes out from my mouth: It will not return to me empty, but will accomplish what I desire and achieve the purpose for which I sent it." (NIV)

The more I grow in Christ, the more I recognize that God is the potter and I am the clay. It's not the other way around. Isaiah 64:8 says, "Yet you, LORD, are our Father. We are the clay, you are the potter; we are all the work of your hand" (NIV).

Who was I to try to order the steps of the Lord? God is the one who orders our every step, regardless of whether we want to accept this truth or deny it. David reminds us in Psalm 37:23, "The steps of a good man are ordered by the LORD" (NKJV).

I am glad the Lord did not rebuke me because of my ignorance and what seems to me now a foolish request. I have to praise God for having mercy on me. Thank you, Jesus!

A Personal Testimony

PERHAPS IT WAS GOOD FOR me to experience that kind of faith when I was a child. Why? Because once I became an adult, I needed my childhood faith—plus more faith in God—to help usher me through some painful experiences I encountered in life.

In 1972 I started experiencing a bad case of chronic depression and a serious bout of mental illness. Unknowingly, I associated myself with several people close to me who were possessed with demonic spirits. They knew how to exploit me mentally, physically, socially, and spiritually. My emotions were turned completely upside down. To say it plainly, I was in a deep pit that felt as if it had no bottom, and I felt I had no way to escape. This demonic attack lasted five years—from October 1972 to October 1977. I knew I was depressed, but I did not know I was suffering from mental illness, nor did I know at that time in my life that mental illness was considered a disability. The doctors did not tell me I had been diagnosed with this kind of illness. They only said to me that I was extremely depressed.

During that time in society, it seemed like people did not talk about mental illness or its status as a disability, perhaps because the term *mentally ill*, as I knew it then, was always associated with the stigma that a person was crazy and belonged in a mental institution. I carried this thought with me far into my adult years. Years later, I finally realized this perception of mental illness was not the whole truth.

Doctor's Confession

I REMEMBER CLEARLY SOMETHING MY doctor said to me during a therapy session. He told me that my condition was so critical that he thought he was going to lose me. I wasn't sure what he meant by that statement at that particular time in my life, because I was too busy working on sorting things out in my life. Only years later—after many sessions of sorting things out and healing my mind, spirit, and body—did I realize what he'd meant. He had been afraid I was going to deteriorate instead of getting better mentally.

When I was enlightened about his statement, I was surprised. I had never felt that way, even during those critical years in my life. You see, I did not consider my maladies as illnesses or even inward threats to harm myself. I viewed them as challenges for me to overcome. Within my spirit, I knew that God and I were going to fight this battle inwardly together. I use the word *inwardly* because no one really knows what is in a person's heart or mind. An individual could never measure another person's faith in God or relationship with God. Only the Lord knows the hearts of all men and what is in an individual's mind. In my heart and mind, I believed in the Word of God and the healing power of Jesus Christ. I held on to the words of Isaiah 53:5 about our healing in Jesus Christ:

> But he was pierced for our transgressions, he was crushed for our iniquities; the punishment that brought us peace was upon him, and by his wounds we are healed (NIV).

With these words embedded in my spirit and mind, I realized that my faith in God's Word was stronger than my disabilities. My entire being was in a bent-over condition. I knew deep down in my soul, beyond the deep pit I was in, that I was already healed, even though the healing process had not yet manifested itself in my body.

Some years later, my therapist commended me for my faith in God. He said, "Thelma, your faith in God brought you through some very difficult times in your life. I didn't think you were going to make it. What you experienced in life would have caused some people to take their lives. God honored your faith, and He will continue doing so because of your strong belief in Him. You are a conqueror and an example that nothing is too hard for God." My doctor, who was Jewish, never gave up on me, because he had a solid faith in God according to his religious beliefs and upbringing.

Rock Bottom

BY NOW, YOU MIGHT BE wondering what caused me to hit rock bottom in my life. What put me in a bent-over condition? What prevented me from immediately standing straight up? I believe my illness was caused by being naive during my two failed marriages. In both marriages, my late husbands were unfaithful. The second marriage was worse than the first. The second marriage almost pushed me over the edge of losing my mind.

My second late husband had many good attributes. He was a good provider and hard worker and was intelligent, but there was another side to him. He knew how to exploit my mind, disrespect me, and strip me of my identity without me realizing it. When I confronted him about his unfaithfulness, he refused to end his adulterous relationship. For the next ten years after confronting him, I lived with a controlling and unfaithful husband who did nothing to stop hurting me and tearing our family apart. His actions almost destroyed me, because I had been faithful to him. I watched my family fall apart because he refused to give up his affair, which added to the mental turmoil I was going through.

Unknowingly, I also allowed wicked and evil people to play games with my mind, which made matters worse for me. I did not know that some of my acquaintances were evil and secretly practiced witchcraft and other secret or dark arts. I was too naive to see it and lacked a spirit of discernment.

Merriam-Webster's Collegiate Dictionary defines *witchcraft* as "the use of sorcery or magic; communication with the devil or with a familiar; an irresistible influence or fascination."[6] *Nelson's Bible Dictionary* says,

> The practice of witchcraft, or divination, was a means for extracting information or guidance from a pagan god. The word describes the activity of Balaam the soothsayer, or professional prophet, who was hired to curse Israel (Numbers 22:7; 23:23; Joshua 13:22). It also describes the woman at En Dor who brought the spirit of Samuel up from the grave. All the major prophets condemned divination (Isaiah 44:25; Jeremiah 27:9; 29:8; Ezekiel 13:9).[7]

Once I discovered what these manipulative people were doing, I did not know how to defend myself. My enemies had learned how to take my spirit of meekness for weakness. They knew how to abuse my kindness. In fact, I believed they sat on their beds of ivory and figured out how to exploit me physically, mentally, socially, and

---

[6] *Merriam Webster's Collegiate Dictionary*, 10th ed., s.v. "witchcraft."

[7] *Nelson's Illustrated Bible Dictionary* Nashville, (Thomas Nelson, 1986).

spiritually. I lost my joy in the Lord and felt as if they'd stripped me of my total being. What puzzled me was how I'd accepted these individuals into my life and treated them with kindness.

If I had done something to cause them some kind of harm or pain or had disrespected them, then maybe I would have understood their actions toward me. I knew then, just as I know now, that I am not a perfect person. I have faults, just as everyone else does, but I was not the kind of person who would purposely cause harm to anyone. Through the years, I learned that you don't have to do anything harmful to an individual in order for him or her to bring harm upon you. Some people will go to the extreme of hurting you just because they are jealous, wicked, envious, or divisive individuals.

Throughout my life, I was always taught to love all of humanity because there is some bad in the best of us and some good in the worst of us. I always try to look for the good in people and not the worst. By doing this, I can stay focused on loving my fellow man. This is what I did then, and I still believe in taking this approach today with the help of the Holy Spirit and the gift of discernment. If I looked for the worst in my brothers and sisters, I would not love them; instead, I would be bitter toward them. I am a firm believer in Mark 12:30–31:

"Love the Lord your God with all your heart and with all your soul and with all your mind and with all your strength … Love your neighbor as yourself. There is no commandment greater than these" (NIV).

A Taste of Bitterness

IF YOU ARE WONDERING IF I became bitter against my enemies, the answer is yes. Not only did I become bitter against my enemies, but also, there were times in my fleshly mind when I wanted to get even. Sometimes I felt God was too slow in chastising my enemies in the way I believed He should punish them. I thought of some ungodly ways to get even with my enemies, but I was too afraid to do something that would land me in jail. Yes, there were many times when sin was ruling in my spirit and mind. It was hard to keep before me the notion that vengeance belonged to God and not to me. I had to work hard on remembering this biblical truth. I thank God that His ways are not like our ways and that His thoughts are not like our thoughts (Isaiah 55:8). I praise Him for not consuming me after my sins, because I deserved it. So yes, in all honesty, I have to admit there were times when I became bitter against my enemies. Whenever I found myself getting bitter in my spirit, I had to exercise the mandate of God's Word recorded in 1 John 1:9–10, which applies to all sin in thought, word, or deed. John tells us:

> If we confess our sins, he is faithful and just and will forgive us our sins and purify us from all unrighteousness. If we claim we have not sinned, we make him out to be a liar and his word has no place in our lives (NIV).

Well, I wanted God's Word to have a place in my life. Therefore, when I felt bitterness rise up in my spirit, I had to exercise my faith in God and pray extremely hard and long to God, asking Him not to let my bitterness turn into hatred. I had to love my enemies in spite of their actions toward me.

The Spirit of Forgiveness

YOU MIGHT BE WONDERING IF I forgave my enemies. The answer is yes, even though there were times when I felt bitter and wanted to get even with my enemies. But I knew that revenge was not God's way. What helped me overcome the spirit of bitterness and take on the spirit of forgiveness was the Word of God. I could not allow my spirit of bitterness to turn into a spirit of hatred and lack of forgiveness. God's Word tells us to love our enemies and pray for those who persecute us (Matthew 5:44). This is difficult to do sometimes. Love, when we feel bitter, is not our focus, because we'd rather get even; we don't want to pray or love but to get even with those who hurt us. Nevertheless, we are commanded to carry out this mandate of love in our lives. No matter how difficult it is to love and pray for our enemies, it is not impossible to accomplish with the help of the Holy Spirit. If we think about God's grace, we will realize that God causes His sun to shine on the evil and the good and sends rain on the righteous and the unrighteous (Matthew 5:45). What helped me overcome the spirit of bitterness and keep it from turning into hatred were the following words Jesus said about forgiveness in the gospel of Matthew:

> Then Peter came to Jesus and asked, "Lord, how many times shall I forgive my brother or sister who sins against me? Up to seven times?" Jesus answered, "I tell you, not seven times, but seventy-seven times." (Matthew 18:21–22 NIV)

This command was a hard order for me to follow, because I had to forgive my enemies not just seven times but 490 times. In other words, the number of times I had to forgive my enemies was an unlimited number of times in a day—not in a year; but in a day. I had to work hard on this biblical command because I had a whole lot of forgiving to do, particularly when trying to get past all the pain my enemies had inflicted upon me. Nevertheless, this is a command for every human being to fulfill, no matter how much harm a person causes us. Remember: with God, all things are possible.

Jesus talks about forgiveness again in Matthew 6:14–15: For if you forgive other people when they sin against you, your heavenly Father will also forgive you. But if you do not forgive others their sins, your Father will not forgive your sins (NIV).

I had to turn these words over and over in my mind because I wanted God to forgive my sins. I didn't want to feel like God did not forgive me when I committed a sin. I couldn't live with that kind of guilt on my mind. Even though I had to learn how to love my enemies, which was hard for me, there was one thing I did not have to do: love their evil deeds. I thank God for the presence and power of the Holy Spirit. He taught me how to love my enemies and how to constantly pray for them. Jesus tells us in Matthew 5:43–45,

> You have heard that it was said, "Love your neighbor and hate your enemy." But I tell you: Love your enemies and pray for those who persecute you, that you may be sons of your Father in heaven. He causes his sun to rise on the evil and the good, and sends rain on the righteous and the unrighteous. (NIV)

Since I've been born again by the power of the Holy Spirit and have been purchased by the blood of Jesus Christ, I have grown wiser through the years. God elevated my naive mind and replaced it with the gift of "discerning of spirits" (1 Corinthians 12:10 NKJV), a gift I never possessed prior to my conversion experience in Christ Jesus. God's grace was sufficient then and is still sufficient to keep me in my life today. If not for God's grace and mercy, I would be like a ship without a sail. If not for God's grace, the waves of sin, shame, and death would consume me. If not for God's grace, I would be heading for the pitfalls of hell and not for the Promised Land. I must echo the words of the psalmist:

> Give thanks to the LORD, for he is good. His love endures forever (Psalm 136:1 NIV).

> It was good for me to be afflicted so that I might learn your decrees (Psalm 119:71 NIV).

All That Medicine

As a result of my illness, my doctor put me on two types of medications: antidepressants and tranquilizers. I was taking eight pills a day, as prescribed by my doctor, for five years: four Elavil fifty milligrams each, and four Valium, ten milligrams each. I did not want to take all of this medication on a daily basis, because it controlled my total being. It affected how I walked, talked, looked, and functioned, which gave my enemies more ammunition to use against me. The more I stayed in this medicated state of mind, the more my enemies planned to destroy me. When I became tired of taking the medicine prescribed to me, I prayed God would deliver me from these drugs.

When I reflect on this period in my life, I wonder how the woman with the bent-over condition in Luke's gospel survived her disability for eighteen long years. The narrative in Luke 13:10–17 does not tell us about the medical process she went through in seeking a cure for her malady. Thinking about her story raises some questions about what she might have gone through during those eighteen years. Did the people in her neighborhood reject her because of her bent-over condition? How did the churchgoers treat her when she entered the synagogue? Was she considered an outcast in society? Was she on any medication during those years? If so, how much medicine did she have to take before she realized the doctors could no longer treat her? Did a doctor ever hospitalize her because of her illness? Mentally, how did she handle her sickness? How did her illness affect her emotionally, socially, and spiritually? The Word of God does not tell us about the woman's eighteen-year process, yet it is clear in God's Word that Jesus miraculously set her free from her infirmity. He put His hand on her, and immediately, she straightened up and praised God. Wow, what a testimony!

When I think about the process I experienced during those five years, sometimes it makes me tremble. I made five attempts at taking myself off of all my medicines. As a result of my efforts, I landed in the hospital each time. My hospital stays lasted at least two to three weeks at a time. The doctor never told me that I had landed in the hospital because I was going through a withdrawal process after stopping all of my medicine at the same time. He only said that I needed to rest and that they had to get my medication levels back to normal again in my system. Well, what did the word *normal* mean regarding my situation? There was nothing normal to me about the amount of medicine I was taking and how it controlled my mind and body. If I'd had to take it only for a short period of time, maybe I would have understood it, but eight psychotropic pills every day for five years? That did not make any sense to me. Since I had no clue what was happening to me in the spiritual realm,

I just kept taking all those pills. I was a walking zombie, functioning off of prescribed drugs. I became addicted to the medication without realizing it. In short, I was a legalized drug addict or substance user. Whatever you want to call it, I became addicted to the medication. The Devil played with my mind, victimized my health, destroyed my marriage and my family, and killed my spirit. He had me in a bent-over condition. I was stuck with disabilities that almost took my life. Satan wanted to sift me like wheat (Luke 22:31). He almost succeeded, but God had another plan for my life. Satan cannot do anything to me or to you that God does not give him and his demons permission to do in my life or in yours. Regardless of what my experiences were like, I had to learn how to forgive my enemies and love them in spite of their actions towards me.

When we read Job chapters 1 and 2, we discover how God gave Satan permission to destroy everything Job had except his life. That was one boundary Satan could not cross over. He could go only as far as God allowed him to go.

> The LORD said to Satan, "Very well, then, everything he has is in your power, but on the man himself do not lay a finger" … Then the LORD said to Satan, "Have you considered my servant Job? There is no one on earth like him; he is blameless and upright, a man who fears God and shuns evil. And he still maintains his integrity, though you incited me against him to ruin him without any reason." "Skin

for skin!" Satan replied. "A man will give all he has for his own life. But stretch out your hand and strike his flesh and bones, and he will surely curse you to your face. The LORD said to Satan, "Very well, then, he is in your hands; but you must spare his life." (Job 1:12; 2:3–6 NIV)

The Bible says that Job was a perfect and upright man. He feared God and avoided evil. He was listed among the biblical characters as one of the wealthiest men in the east. He had a wife, seven sons, and three daughters. Job owned land and had servants, seven thousand sheep, three thousand camels, five thousand yoke of oxen, five hundred she asses, and a large household. However, God took down His divine hedge from around Job and all he held dear to him and allowed Satan to touch all of his possessions, including his family. The Sabeans killed his servants. The animals he used for plowing his field were taken away. Lightning destroyed his sheep. The Chaldeans stole his camels. A tornado swept away the lives of his children, and his body was afflicted with sores. Job, a perfect and upright man, was afflicted above and beyond measure.

Just as God, through His permissive will, allowed Satan to take away everything in Job's life, afflict his body, and encourage his wife to tell Job to "curse God and die" (Job 2:9), likewise, through His permissive will, God allowed the Devil to touch my life. Through His permissive will, God also allowed Satan to touch the life of the woman diagnosed with "a spirit of infirmity" in Luke 13:10–17.

When the ruler of the synagogue became indignant against Jesus because He'd healed the woman with the bent-over condition on the Sabbath, Jesus said to the ruler, "Then should not this woman, a daughter of Abraham, whom Satan has kept bound for eighteen long years, be set free on the Sabbath day from what bound her?" (Luke 13:16 NIV).

God has a divine purpose and blueprint for each one of us. The plans He has for you are different from the plans He has for me. He said in Jeremiah 29:11, "'For I know the plans I have for you,' declares the LORD, 'plans to prosper you and not to harm you, plans to give you hope and a future'" (NIV).

Nevertheless, whatever God's individual blueprints are for our lives, they are designed for our good, for our salvation, and for God's glory. We are here to do His will; it is not the other way around. We had absolutely no part in creating the world and all that is in it. God said in Isaiah 45:12, "It is I who made the earth and created mankind upon it" (NIV).

God is love, and He has a purpose for everything that happens to us, whether good or bad, happy or sad, pleasant or unpleasant. Regardless of what I was experiencing in my life, I remembered what the apostle Paul said in Romans 8:28: "And we know that in all things God works for the good of those who love him, who have been called according to his purpose" (NIV).

During those five years, I had to think about this truth, especially during my last stay in the hospital in August 1977.

Inaccurate Diagnosis

MY LAST STAY IN THE hospital lasted about three weeks. This time, because of the symptoms I was manifesting, the doctor thought I'd had a heart attack. After taking test after test, the doctors could not find anything physically wrong with me. Therefore, it was difficult for them to diagnose my medical condition. They determined that I had muscle spasms of the heart, even though they could not find any medical or physical evidence supporting this diagnosis. When the doctor released me from the hospital, I continued taking eight pills a day, plus two doses of nitroglycerin. I couldn't figure out why they had given me nitroglycerin, especially since they didn't have an accurate medical diagnosis for me. If you were to ask me today how I was able to function as a normal human being, I would tell you it was only by the grace of God and the power of the Holy Spirit.

Since the doctor could not heal me, the only thing I could do was keep reading the Word of God and praying that the Lord would heal me of my malady and deliver me from the psychotropic pills and my wicked enemies. I was sick with a condition that was physically different but not spiritually different from the disability of the woman in Luke's gospel. I needed God to save me from my sins, just as the woman who was bowed together had. I had a bent-over condition and a spiritual malady for five years. There was no way I could straighten myself up. I was looking for a cure and could not find one.

A Breakthrough

Two months after my last stay in the hospital, a traveling evangelist came to town. She prophesied to me and stated some things about me that I knew no one could have told her. We had never laid eyes on each other before that day. She named my enemies and told me they had bound my spirit, mind, and body with a spirit of depression by using a spirit of witchcraft. These spirits were controlling my mind and being. As I mentioned earlier, I had no idea I had surrounded myself with people who practiced witchcraft and related arts. It is extremely important for us to understand that our enemies look and act just like everybody else. They are cunning and deceitful. They go to church with us. They live with us. They work with us. They eat with us. They laugh with us. They socialize with us. They take care of us. They sleep with us. They bless us and curse us. They even transform themselves before us as angels of light. No wonder the apostle Paul tells us in 2 Corinthians 11:14, "And no marvel; for Satan himself is transformed into an angel of light" (KJV).

I was spiritually blind to Satan's devices and ways.

After hearing what the evangelist prophesied to me, I hurried home and started searching the Word of God on the topics of demons and witchcraft. As I researched these two subjects in the Bible, I never thought that someone would have actually bound me with such spirits. During my childhood years, I was taught that God is love and that the Devil is evil. I was never taught just how demonic the Devil is and the kinds of wicked devices he uses to influence people's minds and destroy their lives. I knew that Satan would try to influence me to disobey God, but I did not know, nor could I have even fathomed, in my mind was how evil he is. I knew the difference between good and bad but did not know about evil, witchcraft, and deceptive spirits.

When I read Deuteronomy 18:10–12; 2 Kings 9:22; 2 Chronicles 33:6; Micah 5:12; Nahum 3:4; and Galatians 5:19–20 with an open mind, I believed the Word of God. As you read the following Scripture, ask God to give you spiritual insight and understanding. After you read the verses written below, in your private time with God, research God's Word for yourself. Use a Bible dictionary and a regular dictionary to research the italicized words. During your research, ask the Holy Spirit to open your eyes so that you may behold wonderful things out of His Word. I also encourage you to believe God's Word.

> Let no one be found among you who sacrifices his son or daughter in the fire, who practices *divination* or *sorcery*, interprets *omens*, engages in *witchcraft*, or casts *spells*, or who is a *medium* or *spiritist* or who *consults* the dead.

Anyone who does these things is detestable to the LORD, and because of these detestable practices the LORD your God will drive out those nations before you. (Deuteronomy 18:10–12 NIV)

"How can there be peace," Jehu replied, "as long as all the idolatry and witchcraft of your mother Jezebel abound?" (2 Kings 9:22 NIV)

He sacrificed his children in the fire in the Valley of Ben Hinnom, practiced divination and witchcraft, sought omens, and consulted mediums and spiritists. He did much evil in the eyes of the LORD, arousing his anger. (2 Chronicles 33:6 NIV)

All because of the wanton lust of a prostitute, alluring, the mistress of *sorceries*, who enslaved nations by her prostitution and peoples by her witchcraft. (Nahum 3:4 NIV)

I will destroy your witchcraft and you will no longer cast spells. (Micah 5:12 NIV)

When I read about the works of the flesh in Galatians 5:19–20, which says, "Now the works of the flesh are manifest, which are these; adultery, fornication, uncleanness, lasciviousness, idolatry, witchcraft, hatred, variance, emulations, wrath, strife, seditions, heresies" (KJV), I was convinced of this truth and believed what the evangelist had prophesied to me. As I read the Word of God, the Holy Spirit enlightened my spiritual insight. I believed and accepted the Word of God as true. At that point in my life, I knew only Jesus could deliver me from my physical malady, spiritual bondage, mental disability, and sin-sick soul. I had a "bent-over condition that needed to be straightened up.

During the week the evangelist was in town, I communed with her every day. Each day, she fed me with more wisdom and knowledge from God's Word. Before the week was over, she gave a three-day revival in a hotel conference room. I attended the revival every night, even though I did not want to attend the last service. I was mentally drained from everything the evangelist had disclosed to me that week. When I told her I was not going to attend the last service, she said, "You have to come. You have to receive your blessing tonight. God wants to bless you." I had no idea what she was talking about, but out of obedience, I attended the service on the last night of the revival.

Well, on that Saturday night in October 1977, God delivered me from those eight pills a day and the nitroglycerin. I was slain in the Spirit by the power of God. While I was in the Spirit, I experienced a radical, supernatural miracle and healing through the power of Jesus Christ. The infinite love of God touched me to the core of my being. I have seen spiritual things according to God's Word that are indescribable. I was fellowshipping with Jesus in heavenly places. I did not want to come out of the radical, supernatural mountaintop encounter with God that I experienced through the power of the Holy Spirit.

First Witness

IMMEDIATELY FOLLOWING MY ENCOUNTER WITH God, through the power of the Holy Spirit, several unusual things happened to me within five days. The first experience happened when I returned home that evening from the last night of the revival. At that time, I was married. My husband looked at me and asked, "What happened to you?"

My response was "What do you mean what happened to me?" I thought that was a strange question for him to ask me.

He repeated the question again: "What happened to you?" He saw something different about me when I came home that evening—only God knows what.

All I could say was "I met Jesus tonight. He delivered me, healed me, and saved me." He didn't know how to respond to my answer, but there were some things I knew I wasn't going to allow him to do to me anymore, regardless of how many good qualities he possessed. I was not going to allow him to control me, strip me of my character, belittle me in the presence of people, and exploit my new found faith in Jesus Christ. My eyes were no longer shut; they were wide open. I could see clearly now because an intrinsic change had taken place in my soul. I knew from that day on that I was a changed individual.

Second Witness

THE SECOND INCIDENT OCCURRED ON the following day when I went to church. As I entered the Sunday school class, our interim pastor looked at me and said, "I think Sister Gilbert has something to tell us before we start our class."

Here we go again, I thought. It seemed like another strange statement to me, but this time, it had come from the interim pastor. I had no idea what he was talking about. Therefore, I responded, "I have something to say to you?"

He said yes and then repeated his previous statement: "I think Sister Gilbert has something to tell us before we start our class." Whatever he saw different about me that morning, again, only God knows. I had not told anyone in church other than my husband what had happened to me on Saturday. All I could think to say to everyone in the class was "I met Jesus last night. He delivered me, healed me, and saved me." I felt like people were looking at me as if I had two heads on my shoulders. After making this statement, I took my seat. No one asked me any questions. I knew I had changed on the inside, but I did not realize the change had manifested itself outwardly.

Third Witness

To TOP ALL OF THIS off, the third experience occurred during my doctor's appointment that following Wednesday with the same doctor who'd prescribed my medication. When I entered his office, he looked at me in a puzzled way and said, "Thelma, you look different today."

My response to him was "What do you mean I look different today?"

He said, "You just look different today. What happened?"

I said, "I stopped taking all the medication you prescribed me."

He looked at me again and said, "Thelma, you must pray a lot."

My response was "I don't know about praying a lot, but I do know Jesus delivered me from all those pills I took for five long years, healed me, and saved me."

He did not know what to say after that response. But there was one thing I knew that he did not yet know: he wasn't going to submit any more insurance claims to the insurance company for services he rendered to me. All of his paychecks from the insurance company for my doctor visits had ended. I was not signing my newfound faith and spirit away to the doctor or any insurance company. That was my last visit with that particular doctor, because the blood of Jesus, through the power of the Holy Spirit, had healed, delivered, and saved me. Isaiah was correct when he said in Isaiah 53:5, "By his wounds we are healed" (NIV).

Finally, I'd had my radical, supernatural experience with God. His infinite love is just that—infinite, unlimited, immeasurable. I had had my own personal Damascus Road experience with Jesus Christ. During that encounter, the Holy Spirit had revealed some heavenly things to me from the Word of God. I felt I could identify a little bit with one of the apostle Paul's radical, supernatural encounters with God. Paul said,

> I know a man in Christ who fourteen years ago was caught up to the third heaven. Whether it was in the body or out of the body I do not know—God knows. And I know that this man—whether in the body or apart from the body I do not know, but God knows—was caught up to paradise and heard inexpressible things, things that no one is permitted to tell. I will boast about a man like that, but I will not boast about myself, except about my weaknesses. (2 Corinthians 12:2–5 NIV)

At that point in my life, the Holy Spirit started teaching me some holy common sense. Ones who practice witchcraft, root workers, demons, and all the rest of the demonic hosts cannot harm me anymore. I know they are going to try, but there is a difference now: they will lose the battle. Why? Because Scripture says the following:

> If God is for us, who can be against us? (Romans 8:31 NIV)

> We are more than conquerors through him who loved us. (Romans 8:37 NIV)

> For everyone born of God overcomes the world. This is the victory that has overcome the world, even our faith. (1 John 5:4 NIV)

> But thanks be to God! He gives us the victory through our Lord Jesus Christ. (1 Corinthians 15:57 NIV)

Jesus Christ is omnipotent. He is sovereign. He is Lord. He is the Great Physician. He is Jehovah Ropheka, which means "the Lord is (my) healer."

I do not know what my former husband, the interim pastor, or the doctor saw when I was in their presence, but whatever it was, God was with me. Maybe it was that bright halo I had asked Jesus to place around my head many years earlier. To this day, I still cannot tell you what they saw, but I do know that I was not suspended up in the air in the midst of the congregation.

I promised God that from that point on in my life, I would serve Him until the day I died. I asked God to use me to help His daughters, serve Him and humanity, and witness to a dying world that Jesus can save. I asked Him to heal and deliver us from our spiritual disabilities of sin and from any other kinds of bent-over physical conditions in our lives.

As I was writing this short version of my testimony, I thought about David. He was hurt when he discovered that his own acquaintances had hurt him. He said in Psalm 55:12–14,

> If an enemy were insulting me, I could endure it; if a foe were rising against me, I could hide. But it is you, a man like myself, my companion, my close friend, with whom I once enjoyed sweet fellowship at the house of God, as we walked about among the worshipers. (NIV)

Jesus said in Matthew 10:36, "A man's enemies will be the members of his own household" (NIV).

I could relate to David's testimony and the words of Jesus. As I stated in my personal testimony, members of my own household and close friends had devastated my life. My adversaries turned my life upside down for five years. But God delivered me from my enemies. I believed the Word of God and discovered that God is true to His Word. He is faithful, and His mercy endures forever.

Perhaps members of your household or your close friends bruised you. Maybe they betrayed a trust, damaged your character, abandoned you, or rejected you for one reason or another. Perhaps you qualified for a promotion, but the position was given to someone who did not qualify for it or deserve it. Maybe your spouse had a controlling spirit or was unfaithful to you. Perhaps a member of your family, a close friend, or someone you did not know abused you physically, emotionally, or sexually. Maybe you were mugged or raped while traveling from one place to another, abused by one of your colleagues, or abandoned by your biological parents. Whatever the situation was—or maybe is at this present time in your life—please believe the Word of God. Seek God's face, and draw near to Him. God will draw near to you. David said in Psalm 34:4, "I sought the LORD, and he answered me; he delivered me from all my fears" (NIV). Solomon said in Proverbs 16:7, "When the LORD takes pleasure in anyone's way, he causes their enemies to make peace with them" (NIV).

Remember, the Bible tells us in Deuteronomy 32:35 that vengeance belongs to the Lord: "Vengeance is Mine, and recompense; Their foot shall slip in due time; For the day of their calamity is at hand, And the things to come hasten upon them" (NKJV).

God does not need our help when it comes to getting even with our enemies. He will reward our enemies according to their evil deeds.

Jesus commands us in the book of Luke, "Men always ought to pray and not lose heart" (Luke 18:1 NKJV), and "Be always on the watch, and pray" (Luke 21:36 NIV).

Jesus watched and prayed. He knew who His enemies were. Judas Iscariot was one of His disciples who dined with Him and walked with Him. But Judas also betrayed Jesus for thirty pieces of silver. Matthew 26:14–16 says,

Then one of the Twelve—the one called Judas Iscariot—went to the chief priests and asked, "What are you willing to give me if I hand him over to you?" So they counted out for him thirty silver coins. From then on Judas watched for an opportunity to hand him over. (NIV)

Everyone has enemies, knowingly or unknowingly. You have enemies, and I have enemies—and they are seeking opportunities to destroy you and me. Even Jesus had enemies. The ruler in Luke's narrative was one of Jesus's enemies (Luke 13:14–15). The Pharisees were Jesus's enemies. When Jesus healed a demon-possessed man who was blind and mute so that he could see and talk, the people who witnessed the miracle were astonished. But the Pharisees accused Jesus of demon possession. They said, "It is only by Beelzebub, the prince of demons, that this fellow drives out demons" (Matthew 12:24 NIV).

The Word of God does not say that Jesus was actually called Beelzebub, but he was charged with being in league with Satan and with being possessed by a devil or demon. The people said to Jesus in John 7:20, "You have a demon. Who is seeking to kill you?" (NKJV).

Therefore, we need to carefully observe the type of people we hold company with. Sometimes it is difficult to know who is for you and who is against you.

A friend or a member of your own household can become your worst enemy. I can testify to this truth. I believe many people are sick today with bent-over conditions, just like

I was during those five years, and like the daughter of Abraham in Luke's story, who suffered with her malady for eighteen years, the majority do not even know why they are sick. Their sicknesses are not necessarily due to sin but to demonic forces flying loose in this evil world and in the spiritual realm. I had enemies in my life who were working against me, but I was spiritually blind to their actions. The damage was already done. I was walking around with my eyes wide opened shut, meaning; my eyes were open, but I was not seeing clearly. I was naive. I was spiritually blind and lacked spiritual discernment. My eyes were not spiritually opened until Jesus saved and delivered me, at which point I received the spirit of discernment and really started experiencing the Word of God in and through my life.

If you are sick and the doctors can't heal you, maybe you are naive, or perhaps you have a spiritual disability called sin that is causing you to be spiritually blind. If you are sick and cannot get well, let me encourage you to observe the people involved in your life; examine your relationship with God, your lifestyle, and your environment. You might be in a demonic spiritual battle that is preventing you from fighting back, but you might not know it, because you are too close to see it. Ask God to open your eyes so that you can behold amazing revelations from His Holy Word.

A Spiritual Battle

PAUL TELLS US IN EPHESIANS 6:12, "For our struggle is not against flesh and blood, but against the rulers, against the authorities, against the powers of this dark world and against the spiritual forces of evil in the heavenly realms" (NIV).

God delivered me from my bent-over condition involving chronic depression, mental illness, and people with demonic spirits. He has the same power to deliver you from any malady you are struggling with in your life. Nothing is impossible with God. Jesus said in Matthew 19:26, "With man this is impossible, but with God all things are possible" (NIV).

Thank you, Jesus, for saving me! Thank you for delivering me from chronic depression and mental illness and from the hands of those who practiced the secret art of witchcraft. Thank you for delivering me out of the hands of my enemies. It is my hope and prayer that my testimony will help the person reading this book and enlighten others. We must always keep before us what the Word of God tells us in 2 Corinthians 10:3–5:

For though we live in the world, we do not wage war as the world does. The weapons we fight with are not the weapons of the world. On the contrary, they have divine power to demolish strongholds. We demolish arguments and every pretension that sets itself up against the knowledge of God, and we take captive every thought to make it obedient to Christ. (NIV)

The Christian life is a spiritual walk. In that walk, we will encounter spiritual battles; as Christians, we will not escape them. We can fight these battles only through the power and presence of the Holy Spirit working in and through our lives. God has given us the weapons we need to become victorious over our enemies. He gave us His Word, His presence, and His power. He gave us the vehicle of prayer to talk with Him, as well as faith, love, hope, and the gift of the Holy Spirit. Though we live in the world in these earthly vessels, we do not wage war in the same way the world does.

We must crucify the affections and lusts of the flesh every day. We must keep the flesh under the power and submission of the Holy Spirit. It would do all of us good to heed the words in 1 John 2:15–17:

Love not the world, neither the things that are in the world. If any man love the world the love of the Father is not in him. For all that is in the world, the lust of the flesh, and the lust of the eyes, and the pride of life, is not of the Father, but is of the world. And the world passeth away, and the lust thereof: but he that doeth the will of God abideth forever. (KJV)

Definitions of a Miracle

Since we are dealing with a miracle recorded in Luke 13:10–17, it would be good to define the word *miracle* using several sources and talk about the reality of demons and Satan. Perhaps this will give us a better understanding of these terms and the narrative and help us apply God's Word in our daily lives.

When I read about the miracles of Jesus, I think about *The American Heritage Dictionary*'s definition of the word *miracle.* The dictionary defines a miracle as, "an event that appears inexplicable by the laws of nature and so is held to be supernatural in origin or an act of God."[8]

Merriam Webster's Collegiate Dictionary gives a clear and concise definition of a miracle:

> "an extraordinary event manifesting divine intervention in human affairs; an extremely outstanding or unusual event, thing, or accomplishment; a divinely natural phenomenon

---

[8] *The American Heritage Dictionary*, s.v. "miracle," accessed July 20, 2015, http://www.overcomeproblems.com/miracles.htm.

experienced humanly as the fulfillment of spiritual laws."[9]

William Taylor defines a miracle as follows:

> a work out of the usual sequence of secondary causes and affects which cannot be accounted for by the ordinary operation of those causes, and which is produced by the agency of God through the instrumentality of one who claims to be his representative, and in confirmation of the message which he brings.[10]

From a biblical standpoint, the term *miracle* describes each of the wonderful phenomena accompanying the Jewish and Christian revelations, especially at critical moments.[11] You can find an example of this in Exodus chapter 14, when Jehovah parted the Red Sea so that the children of Israel could cross over on dry ground to escape their enemies. Another example occurs in Acts chapter 16; when Paul and Silas were placed in prison, one prayed, while the other sang praises unto the Lord. They were in agreement with one another. Paul and Silas believed God could perform the miraculous and knew that all things were possible with God. Because of their belief, the Holy Spirit miraculously delivered them out of the hands of their enemies.

---

[9] *Merriam Webster's Collegiate Dictionary*, 10th ed., s.v. "miracle."

[10] Herbert Lockyer, *All the Miracles of the Bible* (Grand Rapids, Michigan: Zondervan, 1961), 13.

[11] Ibid.

The Biblical conception of a miracle is that of extraordinary work of deity, transcending the ordinary powers of nature and wrought in connection with the beginning and ends of revelation. Bible miracles often display the reversal of nature's course. Miracles form an effect contrary to the established constitution and course of things. Many of the miracles are sensible deviation from the known laws of nature, proving that God is not only the Maker of all these laws, but also their Sovereign, and consequently He is able to deal with them as He deems fit.[12]

After all, God is the Creator of the universe. Genesis 1:1 and Psalm 24:1 document this truth as follows, respectively: "In the beginning God created the heavens and the earth" (NIV) and "The earth is the LORD's, and everything in it, the world, and all who live in it" (NIV).

Therefore, in biblical miracles, original laws were not suspended, violated, or modified in any way, but a supernatural power outside of nature intervened with a new effect. Having created what we call nature, God has the power to control, change, suspend, or direct its laws for a season, according to His holy will, which is always good and just. David Hume, a Scottish philosopher, puts it this way: "A miracle is not a violation of the laws of nature but the introduction of a new agent."[13]

---

[12] Ibid. 13–14.
[13] Ibid. 14.

We must always remember that since God is beyond and above nature, He never violates any of its laws. Neither is nature, as Spinoza expresses it, "the strait jacket from which God cannot escape."[14] Trench reminds us, "If we deny Him the power to perform miracles, then He is no longer a God of freedom, a living God, above nature and independent of nature."[15]

Perhaps one could say the term *miracle* refers to what is done, the term *sign* refers to what the miracle points to, and the term *wonder* refers to what the miracle produces in those who witness it.

The evangelist sent to me under the guidance of the Holy Spirit was one of God's representatives. She was empowered by the Holy Spirit, which endowed her with the gifts of healing, deliverance, prophecy, miracles, and more. She brought a message to me from the Lord under the inspiration and power of the Holy Spirit.

---

[14] Ibid.
[15] Ibid.

The Reality of Demons and Satan, or Devils

MANY PEOPLE DENY THE FACT that Satan and his demons are real. Born-again believers in Jesus Christ and students of the Word of God know that Satan is alive and active in the affairs of men. In fact, he is written in the blueprints for our lives. Yet some, including babes in Christ, still ask questions like the following: Are Satan and his demons real? Are there really such things as demons, or devils?

The language of Jesus indicates his own belief in the existence of a personal devil. Jesus knew what He was talking about, especially after His experience with Satan during His forty days in the wilderness (Matthew 4:1–11).

Satan is the arch thief of the universe in relation to both God and man. He seems to have power of mental suggestion, which can lead to action. In other words, if we allow the Devil to control our minds with thoughts or ideas, eventually, those thoughts or ideas could become realities that we put into action. The only way to hinder a demonic thought or idea is through the Word of God and the power of the Holy Spirit.

The Devil can also invade people's bodies, as in the following Scripture: "As soon as Judas took the bread, Satan entered into him" (John 13:27 NIV). The Devil uses this form of work only on rare occasions and with special individuals—and only by their consent or when they leave an opening for him.[16] I do not know at what age the nameless woman in Luke 13:10–17 became disabled with a bent-over condition or what caused her to inherit this illness. The narrative does not give us this information. However, we know one thing for sure: there was an open door that allowed Satan to afflict her for eighteen long years.

Satan's influence appears more frequently in people's lives through the medium of demons. James 4:7 says, "Submit yourselves, then, to God. Resist the devil, and he will flee from you" (NIV).

---

[16] D. D. Bancroft, *Elemental Theology, Doctrinal and Conservative* (Hayward, California: J. F. May Press, 1948), 264, 269.

Demons

WHEN IT COMES TO THE Scripture, some people are uncertain whether or not to put demons in the same category with evil angels, but since there is positive teaching concerning each, there can be no doubt.

Instead of using the word *devil*, which appears in our English Bible, we should substitute the word *demon*, as the American Standard Revised Version does. *Devil* is the translation of the Greek *diabolos*, meaning "the accuser," a noun used in the singular to Satan, as in John 8:44:

> You belong to your father, the devil, and you want to carry out your father's desire. He was a murderer from the beginning, not holding to the truth, for there is no truth in him. When he lies, he speaks his native language, for he is a liar and the father of lies. (NIV)

Devil is also the translation of the Greek *daimonion*, meaning "demon," or one of the numerous evil spirits left behind to infest the world and cause disasters, especially physical and mental illness.[17]

Jesus recognized demons and their existence by speaking of them and to them. He commanded His disciples to minister especially to those who were maladjusted to life because of demonic domination. The following verses of Scripture demonstrate this truth.

> And if I drive out demons by Beelzebub, by whom do your people drive them out? So then, they will be your judges. But if I drive out demons by the Spirit of God, then the kingdom of God has come upon you. (Matthew 12:27–28 NIV)

> Jesus called his twelve disciples to him and gave them authority to drive out impure spirits and to heal every disease and sickness. (Matthew 10:1 NIV)

> Heal the sick, raise the dead, cleanse those who have leprosy, drive out demons. Freely you have received, freely give. (Matthew 10:8 NIV)

> After this, Jesus traveled about from one town and village to another, proclaiming the good news of the kingdom of God. The Twelve were

---

[17] Madeleine S. Miller and J. Lane, *The New Harper's Bible Dictionary* (New York: Harper and Row, 1890), 136.

with him, and also some women who had been cured of evil spirits and diseases: Mary (called Magdalene) from whom seven demons had come out. (Luke 8:1–2 NIV)

The seventy-two whom Jesus sent out on a mission recognized that demons were real. The seventy-two returned with joy after Jesus sent them to carry out His divine will. They said to Jesus, "Lord, even the demons submit to us in your name" (Luke 10:17 NIV).

The apostle Paul also recognized the reality of demons in his day and gave warning against them. In Acts chapter 16, he cast them out in the name of Jesus Christ.

One of those listening was a woman from the city of Thyatira named Lydia, a dealer in purple cloth. She was a worshiper of God. The Lord opened her heart to respond to Paul's message. When she and the members of her household were baptized, she invited us to her home. "If you consider me a believer in the Lord," she said, "come and stay at my house." And she persuaded us. Once when we were going to the place of prayer, we were met by a female slave who had a spirit by which she predicted the future. She earned a great deal of money for her owners by fortune-telling. She followed Paul and the rest of us, shouting, "These men are servants of the Most High God, who are telling you the way to be saved."

> She kept this up for many days. Finally Paul became so annoyed that he turned around and said to the spirit, "In the name of Jesus Christ I command you to come out of her!" At that moment the spirit left her. (Acts 16:14–18 NIV)

James recognized the existence of demons and accredited them with trembling because of their belief in God: "You believe that there is one God. Good! Even the demons believe that—and shudder" (James 2:19 NIV).

Though demonology can present difficult problems in a person's life, the record of Christianity testifies to the power of the gospel to correct a distorted mental state. Paul shared the conceptions of his day in regard to the personal sources of evil, and made the offerings to heathen gods synonymous with sacrifices to devils.[18] He says in 1 Corinthians 10:20–21,

> No, but the sacrifices of pagans are offered to demons, not to God, and I do not want you to be participants with demons. You cannot drink the cup of the Lord and the cup of demons too; you cannot have a part in both the Lord's table and the table of demon. (NIV)

---

[18] Ibid.

Satan

PEOPLE'S BELIEFS CONCERNING SATAN RANGE from the silly to the abstract—from a little red guy with horns who sits on your shoulder urging you to sin, to an expression used to describe the personification of evil. The Bible, however, gives us a clear portrait of who Satan is and how he affects our lives. Put simply, the Bible defines Satan as an angelic being who fell from his position in heaven due to sin and is now completely opposed to God, doing all in his power to thwart God's purposes.[19]

Satan's name means adversary or accuser. He seeks to destroy our soul and tempt us to disobey God's word. Jesus said to His disciples in John 14:30, "I will not say much more to you, for the prince of this world is coming. He has no hold over me" (NIV).

Here, Jesus referred to Satan as the prince of this world, or the prince of our sinful society. He also recognized him as such during his temptation in the wilderness (Luke 4:5–7), when Satan offered him all of the kingdoms of the world and the glory of them if he would fall down and worship

---

[19] http://www.gotquestions.org/who-Satan.html

him. Jesus defeated Satan in the wilderness experience. Satan tempted Jesus three times, and each time, Jesus used the Word of God to neutralize him. Jesus knew He already possessed the kingdoms Satan was offering Him. By using the Word of God, He was victorious over Satan.

Satan is a great strategist and uses numerous wiles and subtle assaults against us. For this reason, the apostle Paul instructed us to put on the whole armor of God.

> Finally, be strong in the Lord and in his mighty power. Put on the full armor of God so that you can take your stand against the devil's schemes. For our struggle is not against flesh and blood, but against the rulers, against the authorities, against the powers of this dark world and against the spiritual forces of evil in the heavenly realms. (Ephesians 6:10–12 NIV)

If we are not fully dressed in the whole armor of God, we will live defeated lives. If we are clothed with the full armor of God, we will be conquerors through Jesus Christ, our Lord. This is not to say that the woman who had a bent-over condition was not fully armed with the Word of God. She must have been clothed to some degree with God's Word, because she attended the services held at the synagogue on the Sabbath. Perhaps she was going to keep wrestling with God until He blessed her.

Jesus's and the Bible's Statements about the Reality of Satan

JESUS SAID A GREAT DEAL about Satan when the Devil tempted him in the wilderness. He called him "the enemy" (Matthew 13:39); "the evil one" (Matthew 13:38); "a liar" and "the father of lies" (John 8:44); "the prince of the world" (John 12:31; 14:30); and "a murderer" (John 8:44). He said Satan "has a kingdom" (Matthew 12:26); has "fallen from heaven" (Luke 10:18); "has angels" (Matthew 25:41); "sowed tears among the wheat" (Matthew 13:38–39); "snatch[ed] the Word from hearers" (Matthew 13:19); "desire[d] to have Peter" (Luke 22:31); and "bound a woman for eighteen years" (Luke 13:16).[20]

The Bible presents Satan as "the tempter" (Matthew 4:3); "the prince of demons" (Mark 3:22); the "source of demonical possession" (Luke 11:14–23); one who "perverts the Scriptures" (Luke 4:10–11); "the god of this world" (2 Corinthians 4:4); "the prince of the power of the air"

---

[20] H. H. Haley, *Haley Bible Handbook* (Grand Rapids, Michigan: Zondervan, 1965), 497–98.

(Ephesians 2:2); one who "fashions himself into an angel of light" (2 Corinthians 11:14); "our adversary" (1 Peter 5:8); "the deceiver of the world" (Revelation 12:9); "the great dragon, the old serpent" (Revelation 12:9; 20:2); "seducer of Adam and Eve" (Genesis 3:1–20); the "cause of Paul's thorn in the flesh" (2 Corinthians 12:7); the "cause of Ananias to lie" (Acts 5:3); one who "can produce false miracles" (2 Thessalonians 2:9); and the "cause of Job's troubles" (Job 1:7-22; 2:1-10). He "blinds the minds of unbelievers" (2 Corinthians 4:4) and is like "a roaring lion seeking whom he may devour" (1 Peter 5:8). Furthermore, "evil men are his children" (1 John 3:8–10), and he "is overcome by faith" (1 Peter 5:9). "Gentiles are under his power" (Acts 26:17–18). Satan is "the spirit that works in the disobedient" (Ephesians 2:2). He "gets the advantage of Christians" (2 Corinthians 2:11) and "moved David to sin" (1 Chronicles 21:1). "He will flee if resisted" (James 4:7), and "false teachers are a synagogue of Satan" (Revelation 2:9; 3:9). Satan "was the adversary of Joshua" (Zechariah 3:1–9).[21]

---

[21] Ibid., 498.

The Sabbath Miracles of Jesus

JESUS PERFORMED MANY MIRACLES DURING His earthly ministry. The Bible first described his ministry as follows: "Jesus went throughout Galilee, teaching in their synagogues, preaching the good news of the kingdom, and healing every disease and sickness among the people" (Matthew 4:23 NIV). However, teaching, preaching, and healing were only a few aspects of Jesus's earthly ministry. He exercised His God-given power so that men might believe in Him as the true Messiah sent from God. The miracle recorded in Luke 13:10–17 demonstrates a few aspects of Jesus's mission. Teaching in the synagogue on the Sabbath day was not unusual for Jesus. He never hesitated to carry out any part of His divine assignment. Jesus always did what pleased His Father. He taught, preached, and healed, even on the Sabbath, regardless of the opposition He knew He would encounter from His enemies.

However, if we examine the Scriptures, we discover only seven miracles were performed by the Master on the Sabbath day. I've listed the names and scriptural locations of those miracles below.

1. The Impotent Man at Jerusalem (John 5:1–9)
2. The Man Born Blind (John 9:1–14)
3. The Demoniac in Capernaum (Mark 1:21–27; Luke 4:31–37)
4. The Mother-in-Law of Peter (Mark 1:29–31; Matthew 8:14–15; Luke 4: 38–39)
5. The Man with the Withered Hand (Mark 3:1–6; Matthew 12:9–14; Luke 6:6–11)
6. The Man with the Dropsy (Luke 14:1–6)
7. A Woman Bowed Over (Luke 13:10–17)

Perhaps you have realized by now that the Lord moved me to write about the seventh miracle, entitled "A Woman Bowed Over," or "The Woman Who Had a Spirit of Infirmity." I chose to focus on this particular miracle because it relates to the human conditions of mankind. It also involves a woman who had an infirmity for eighteen years, a healing Christ, a complaining ruler, and an elated crowd. Things have not changed since biblical days. Many people living in our society today have been diagnosed with all manner of disabilities. Some were born with disabilities, while others inherited disabilities during the course of their lives. Though some disabilities are not as critical as others, the majority of people who are diagnosed with illnesses normally seek medical help. Whatever the case might be, many people who have disabilities have lost hope and their senses of belonging, direction, and purpose in life. Nevertheless, whatever the loss might be, people with some types of disabilities living in our society today are still seeking cures or medical assistance to help them live comfortable lives free of pain, sorrow, and despondency.

Noticeable and Unnoticeable Maladies

SOME DISABILITIES ARE NOTICEABLE, AND some are not. For example, sometimes it is hard to identify people who have been diagnosed with asthma, fibromyalgia, high blood pressure, diabetes, dyslexia, depression, or mental illness. Many times it is difficult for people to notice that individuals have these types of illnesses, unless the individuals manifest some type of symptom. I am not talking about difficulty for professional people who work in the medical field, such as doctors and nurses; I am talking about observers who do not have the medical expertise to diagnose another individual's illness. For this reason, many disabilities go unnoticed by others. On the other hand, some disabilities, such as blindness or the loss of an arm or leg, are noticeable because the maladies are visible to human eyes.

In the narrative in Luke chapter 13, the woman's illness was noticeable. She "was bent over and could not straighten up." She had been afflicted with this particular condition for eighteen long years. The New King James Version of the Bible says she had "a spirit of infirmity." The New International Version says she "had been crippled by a spirit." The Message Bible states that she was "so twisted and bent over." Her condition was so unbearable that she couldn't even straighten herself up to fully observe her surroundings. Some people today would call this woman a cripple or an invalid or refer to her as deformed, handicapped, abnormal, or different. They would look upon her as if she were an outcast in society—someone without rights, privileges, intelligence, integrity, self-worth, or dignity—instead of a productive citizen in society worthy of respect and acceptance.

A Nameless Woman

THE BIBLE DOES NOT GIVE this woman a first or last name. She is only identified as a "Daughter of Abraham" (Luke 13:16 NIV) whom Satan had bound for eighteen long years. The story mentions nothing about her family history, medical background, or next of kin. Personally, I would like to believe she was a God-fearing woman and a decent human being who not only was disabled but also had three great attributes that many of us lack today: hope, faith in God, and a persistent attitude. The woman's disability did not define who she was as a person; instead, she was defined by her hope, faith in God, and a persistent attitude. Her focus was on Jesus Christ, the Great Physician, who could perform the miraculous. Her mind was not on the people ridiculing her or her surroundings but on the omnipotent healer who could do what no other power could do. This woman demonstrated to us that Jesus could heal anyone who put his or her faith and trust in Jesus's ability to heal his or her infirmity. Mark 3:10–11 tells us that during Jesus's earthly ministry, "he had healed many, so that those with diseases were pushing forward to touch him." Whenever the impure spirits saw him, they fell down before him and cried out, "You are the Son of God" (NIV).

Many people Jesus healed recognized that He was the Son of God. Even the evil spirits knew Jesus was the promised Messiah.

We find a similar situation in Matthew 8:28–31, concerning two men who were possessed with demons. The Word says,

> When he arrived at the other side in the region of the Gadarenes, two demon-possessed men coming from the tombs met him. They were so violent that no one could pass that way. "What do you want with us, Son of God?" they shouted. "Have you come here to torture us before the appointed time?" Some distance from them a large herd of pigs was feeding. The demons begged Jesus, "If you drive us out, send us into the herd of pigs." (NIV)

When you read the next few verses, you will discover what happened. Jesus said, "Go," and the demons left them.

Within the souls of the two men, the demons who possessed the men knew Jesus was omnipotent. They knew the power Jesus had in the palms of His hands. The evil spirits were aware of the fact that Jesus could execute a miracle even when someone merely touched the hem of His garment. The men knew He could do what no other power could do. They believed He could make an eye salve out of clay and saliva to anoint a blind man's eyes so that he could receive his sight. In fact, Jesus didn't need to be in the presence of the person who needed healing.

The writer of Hebrews reminds us that Jesus, is the same yesterday, and today, and forever" (Hebrews 13:8 NIV).

When Jesus healed the centurion's servant, He was not in the servant's presence. He just said the following words to the centurion: "Go! It will be done just as you believed it would." Afterward, "his servant was healed at that very hour" (Matthew 8:13 NIV). The centurion's servant was miraculously healed the same hour that Jesus uttered those words to him.

Jesus still has the same power and ability to heal people today through the power of the Holy Spirit as He did in biblical days. Jesus is immutable—he changes not. And guess what: Jesus has given every blood-washed, born-again child of God the same power to cast out demonic spirits today. Read the words Jesus spoke to His disciples in Mark 16:15–18.

> Go into all the world and preach the gospel to all creation. Whoever believes and is baptized will be saved, but whoever does not believe will be condemned. And these signs will accompany those who believe: In my name they will drive out demons; they will speak in new tongues; they will pick up snakes with their hands; and when they drink deadly poison, it will not hurt them at all; they will place their hands on sick people, and they will get well. (NIV)

We are children of the Most High, and Jesus made it clear to us that He would give His children power. John 1:12 says, "But as many as received him, to them gave he power to become the sons of God, even to them that believe on his name" (KJV).

One important aspect of this miracle is Jesus's ability to heal those who trust Him, have faith in Him, and accept the truth of His Word. Jesus said in John 8:32, "And you shall know the truth and the truth shall make you free" (NKJV).

Just as Jesus performed a miracle on a woman who had been sick and carrying a burden for eighteen long years, He can still deliver us from all kinds of maladies today. We must realize and acknowledge that when Jesus performs a miracle in our lives, it is not for our glory. It is for His glory only. The miracle is for us to place our total trust, faith, and hope in Him no matter what our situation in life looks like.

Not a Name Issue but a Faith Issue

THE MIRACLE IN LUKE 13 is not about the woman's name, her status, where she came from, her family history and their illnesses, or whether she had health insurance. There is nothing in this narrative that indicates she was supported by the state, the city, or relatives. There's no mention of an intake process or a referral from one doctor to another. When we read the narrative, we will notice that Jesus acknowledged the woman's status as a daughter of Abraham. He never called her by her name. Jesus knew that the sickness was not in the woman's name, and neither was it in her status as a daughter of Abraham. The illness was in her body, mind, and spirit. Therefore, her malady was not a name issue but a faith issue. She wasn't looking to be delivered from her name, as many people in our society today are, who pay to have their names changed because they do not like the names given to them at birth. In fact, it seemed as if her name wasn't even important to her. If it was, maybe she would have stated her name to Jesus when He called her "woman" (Luke 13:12, 16). Anyone who has had an illness for a long time is not focusing on his or her name but on how to be released from the malady.

This is also clear in the story about the man at the pool of Bethesda in John 5:1–15, whom Jesus healed of an infirmity he'd had for thirty-eight long years. The man did not have a name. He is referred to as "the man who had an infirmity for thirty eight years" (NIV).

Mark 7:24–30 tells a story about a Syrophoenician woman who had a conversation with Jesus about her demon-possessed daughter. During their conversation, she gathered enough nerve to ask Jesus to heal her daughter and free her from the demon. This story never mentions the names of the woman and her daughter. Nevertheless, Jesus cast out the demon, healed the woman's daughter, and commended the woman on her faith. Jesus said in Mark 7:29, "For such a reply, you may go; the demon has left your daughter" (NIV).

Jesus demonstrated three different methods of healing: (1) speaking to the Syrophoenician woman, (2) being in the presence of the man at the pool of Bethesda, and (3) laying His hand on the woman bound by a spirit of infirmity for eighteen years.

Our nameless woman with the bent-over condition knew that if she was going to continue coping with her terrible illness, her strength and faith had to come from the Word of God. For this woman, the synagogue on the Sabbath day was the right place to be, especially if Jesus was going to be there. She was going to the synagogue to hear a word from the Lord and find comfort for her soul. But when she was in the synagogue, where Jesus was teaching, Jehovah

Ropheka had another plan for her life. Maybe one of the reasons the writer did not give her name in the narrative was because she had a faith issue.

What kind of faith do we have in the ability of Jesus to heal us after the doctors have told us there is nothing else they can do to help us get well again? It is just a matter of time before our lives end. Can we exercise our mustard-seed-sized faith, as this woman did in this story? The Word of God tells us in Matthew 17:20, "I say to you, if you have faith as a mustard seed, you will say to this mountain, 'Move from here to there,' and it will move; and nothing will be impossible for you" (NIV).

Faith: What Is It?

THE WRITER OF HEBREWS SAYS,

> Now faith is the substance of things hoped for,
> the evidence of things not seen … But without
> faith it is impossible to please him: for he that
> cometh to God must believe that he is, and that
> he is a rewarder of them that diligently seek
> him. (Hebrews 11:1, 6 NIV)

Many Christians look at Hebrews 11:1 as the biblical definition of faith. Since the Word of God uses the word *faith* in many different ways, in this verse of Scripture, the word *faith* is not a definition but, rather, a description of faith. Faith has tremendous power because, as I like to say, faith does. Faith is an action word put into practice. If we could see it, touch it, or handle it, then it would not be faith. The word *substance* means "essence" or "reality." Faith treats things hoped for as reality. *Endurance* means "proof" or "conviction." Faith itself proves that what is unseen is real, such as believers being rewarded at the reunion of Jesus Christ. The apostle Paul tells us in 2 Corinthians

4:18, "So we fix our eyes not on what is seen, but on what is unseen. For what is seen is temporary, but what is unseen is eternal" (NIV).

In Hebrews 11:6, the word *comes* is used repeatedly; it refers to the privilege of drawing near to Christ. True faith is a mark of expectancy. The following verses in Hebrews support this fact.

> Let us then approach God's throne of grace with confidence, so that we may receive mercy and find grace to help us in our time of need. (Hebrews 4:16 NIV)

> Therefore he is able to save completely those who come to God through him, because he always lives to intercede for them. (Hebrews 7:25 NIV)

> Let us draw near to God with a sincere heart and with the full assurance that faith brings, having our hearts sprinkled to cleanse us from a guilty conscience and having our bodies washed with pure water. (Hebrews 4:16 NIV)

The writer of Hebrews explains that faith is mandatory for those who approach God, as recorded in chapter 10: "But when this priest had offered for all time one sacrifice for sins, he sat down at the right hand of God" (Hebrews 10:12 NIV)

The word *rewarder* indicates that God rewards only those who seek Him and do good works in the Holy Spirit. Revelation 22:12 says, "Look, I am coming soon! My reward is with me, and I will give to each person according to what they have done" (NIV).

The Daughter of Abraham's Faith

I DO NOT KNOW HOW much faith the woman with the disability had in Jesus's ability to heal her, but I have to believe her faith was at least as "a grain of a mustard seed." Jesus tested her mustard-seed-like faith. I would like to suppose she worked her mustard-seed-like faith to its fullest potential. The Word of God tells us in 2 Corinthians 5:7, "We live by faith, not by sight" (NIV).

Faith believes in God's ability to change things. Faith knows that all things are possible with God.

Since this daughter of Abraham was accustomed to going to the synagogue on the Sabbath, she must have been not only a woman of faith but also a woman of prayer. Maybe she heard Jesus say the following:

> "Have faith in God," Jesus answered. "Truly I tell you, if anyone says to this mountain, 'Go, throw yourself into the sea,' and does not doubt in their heart but believes that what they say will happen, it will be done for them. Therefore I tell you, whatever you ask

for in prayer, believe that you have received
it, and it will be yours. (Mark 11:22–24 NIV)

Or perhaps she heard Him say, "Men ought always to
pray, and not to faint" (Luke 18:1 NIV).

Nevertheless, whatever she heard Jesus say in the
synagogue inspired her to hold fast to her faith. These
verses of Scripture advocate two things every human being
should take part in: faith and prayer. She must have been
a woman of faith and prayer. You can't have one without
the other. Faith and prayer are twins. They are inseparable.
One cannot operate without the other. This woman must
have believed it was a privilege to pray while she was in the
synagogue. An unknown writer said prayer is the "highest
exercise a person can engage in."

Perhaps the prayers of the woman with the spirit of
infirmity are the kinds of prayers that each one of us
needs to pray, not just in a time of need but every day.
She must have offered soul-stirring prayers of persistent
asking, seeking, and knocking until she received an answer
from God (Matthew 7:7–8). Prayer is making our request
known unto God in faith. When it comes to prayer, Paul
admonishes us, "Do not be anxious about anything, but in
every situation, by prayer and petition, with thanksgiving,
present your requests to God" (Philippians 4:6 NIV).

Praying in this way should be the case for every born-
again Christian in the body of Christ. We should have a
constant habit of praying both in and out of season. In
other words, prayer should be a habitual activity in our
lives every day. It should be our meat. It should be our

drink. It should be the substance of our spirit and soul. When things are going well and everything is sweet and running smoothly in our lives, we should still be praying. When things are chaotic in our lives, we should be praying. When we find ourselves facing different adversities in life, including dealing with sickness, death, and problems we cannot solve, we need to be praying. Prayer changes things and people.

If Jesus Prayed, What about Us?

JESUS LEFT AN EXAMPLE FOR us to follow in the area of prayer. Even though He was God and people prayed to Him, He was also a man who prayed. When He was baptized, He was praying (Luke 3:21). When He withdrew into the wilderness, He fasted and prayed (Luke 4:2). There was a time when Jesus went out onto a mountain to pray and continued all night in prayer. Before His transfiguration, Jesus prayed (Luke 9:28–29). In the garden of Gethsemane, the Master prayed (Matthew 26:39). From the cross on Calvary, the Son of God prayed (Luke 23:34). Prayer includes more than just formal church prayers or brief prayers before meals or at bedtime. Prayer is the lifeline to an abundant life in Jesus Christ. All of our Savior's prayers were coupled with faith in His heavenly Father.

The exercise of prayer and faith should be our constant thought, moment by moment and hour by hour. The Word of God tells us, "Continue in prayer, and watch in the same with thanksgiving" (Colossians 4:2 KJV).

When two men dressed in white told the disciples to return to Jerusalem after they witnessed Jesus ascending into heaven before their eyes and a cloud hiding Him, they were obedient to the command. Once they returned to Jerusalem the disciples and the women who were with them, including Mary, the mother of Jesus, went upstairs to a room where they stayed and waited for the promise of the Father (Acts 1:4–13). They did not just sit there doing nothing. The writer does not state that the women were serving the men, nor is there any indication that the men separated themselves from the women. The Word of God tells us in Acts 1:14, "They all joined together constantly in prayer, along with the women and Mary the mother of Jesus, and with his brothers" (NIV).

What an example for us to follow today, individually and collectively. The way the world is shaping up today, group prayer meetings are becoming a lost art. It seems we only pray when things are being turned upside down in our lives instead of praying both in and out of season. We need to pray all the time, regardless of our situation in life. In fact, we are commanded to prayer. Jesus said in Luke 18:1, "Men always ought to pray and not lose heart" (NKJV).

Some unknown writers made the following statements about prayer:

"Prayer is the opening of the skylight of the soul, to the life that is above"[22] and "Prayer is a pouring out of the soul unto God, as a free will offering, solemnly and eternally dedicated to Him."[23]

---

[22] Accessed June 18, 2015, http://www.prayers.org/articles/article_mar03.asp.

[23] Bible Hub, accessed July 16, 2015, http://www.biblehub.com/niv/matthew/6-5.htm.

It is a privilege to pray in faith. I believe the bent-over woman had a prayer life during all of her years of suffering and pain. If this had not been the case, perhaps her prayer life and thanksgiving unto the Lord would not have heightened after Jesus healed her. Luke states in Luke 13:13, "Then he put his hands on her, and immediately she straightened up and praised God" (NIV).

What about you? Are you living a life of prayer as Jesus did? If you are not, then I suggest you start doing so at this moment. Things happen and change when you pray. Souls are saved when you pray. The Devil is conquered when you pray. Healing takes place when you pray. Problems roll away when you pray. Burdens lift when you pray. You receive answers when you pray. Doors open when you pray. There is a saying: "No prayer, no power. Little prayer, little power. Much prayer, much power." Prayer is a privilege. Try it! You'll like it. It works. God might not answer your prayers when you want Him to, but I am a living witness that He will answer your prayers right on time. He answered the prayers of the woman who had a "spirit of infirmity, and He answered my prayers. She had to wait for her change to come, I had to wait for my change to come, and you will have to wait for your change to come. Whatever the case may be in your life today, God will answer your prayers. If the answer is yes, praise God! If the answer is no, still praise God. If the answer is to wait, keep on waiting and praying. God will give you the grace to handle an answer of no, because "His grace is sufficient" (2 Corinthians 12:9).

Satan afflicted the apostle Paul with a thorn in the flesh. At times, it hindered him from serving God and traveling from place to place. I do not know how long he had this affliction, but his desire was for God to remove it. Paul prayed three times for God to remove this disability. God did not grant the apostle his request. Instead, God answered Paul's prayer by telling him, "My grace is sufficient for thee: for my strength is made perfect in weakness" (2 Corinthians 12:9 KJV).

The apostle did not get angry with God; he responded with a positive attitude. He said,

> Most gladly therefore will I rather glory in my infirmities, that the power of Christ may rest upon me. Therefore I take pleasure in infirmities, in reproaches, in necessities, in persecutions, in distresses for Christ's sake: for when I am weak, then am I strong. (2 Corinthians 12:9–10 KJV)

Every blood-washed, born-again child of God should have this same attitude when God's answer is no. If the answer is no, it is for God's divine purpose and for our good. An answer of yes is always easier to accept from God, and a no is more difficult to receive. We must remember what Romans 8:27–28 tells us:

> In the same way, the Spirit helps us in our weakness. We do not know what we ought to pray for, but the Spirit himself intercedes for us with groans that words cannot express. And we know that in all things God works

for the good of those who love him, who have
been called according to his purpose. (NIV)

God is working things out for our good, no matter how
bitter or sweet the journey might be.

Imagine putting yourself in the place of the woman who
had this terrible disability for all those years. She probably
thought God was not going to answer her prayers, but He did
according to His timing and divine purpose. Nevertheless,
she never gave up. Through all those years of suffering with
this terrible illness, she experienced that God's grace was
sufficient to keep her. She prayed and exercised her faith in
God's ability and power to deliver her. Whatever you are
going through in life, no matter how difficult the trial is,
remember that God's grace is sufficient to keep you right
in the midst of your circumstances.

How do I know His grace is sufficient? Because His
grace kept me when I wanted to hear a yes instead of
a no. He kept me when I was going through trials and
tribulations. When I was jobless, His grace was sufficient.
When I was sick, His grace was sufficient. When I lost a
loved one close to me, His grace was sufficient. When I
needed a lawyer, His grace was sufficient. When I had no
money in my pocket or food in my cupboard, His grace
was sufficient. When I went through a terrible divorce, His
grace was sufficient. When my children lay heavy on my
heart, His grace was sufficient. When I became a single
parent after my divorce, His grace was sufficient—and it
is still sufficient to keep me even today.

It's the Name, Not the Disability

WHEN I READ THIS STORY, I thought about my mother's faith in God, persistence, and determination during my childhood and adult years. She demonstrated strength and endurance despite her disability. When she was a child, she was afflicted with polio. She had several operations on her legs over the course of her early childhood years. As a result of the operations, my mother limped when she walked. People identified her not by her name but by her disability. She was the woman who limped. Out of ignorance, many people, including me, have followed this same pattern when we have forgotten someone's name during a conversation with another person. In trying to think of the person's name, we identify the individual in other ways to help the other person realize whom we are speaking about, especially if the person has a disability. We say something like "You know who I am talking about—the woman in the wheelchair," or "She's the woman who limps when she walks." Then the other person responds by saying something like "Yeah, I don't know her name either, but I know who you are speaking about—the handicapped woman," or "Yeah, the lady who limps due to polio." People seldom identified my mother by her name, only by her disability.

If my mother was alive today and I had this conversation with an individual who did not know I was her daughter and identified her by her disability, I would say, "Oh, you are speaking about my mother, Mrs. Simmons. Yes, she has a disability, but her disability is not her name. My mother, Mrs. Simmons, is a great woman who possesses many wonderful characteristics. She is intelligent and full of wisdom, knowledge, integrity, dignity, and strength. She has a great sense of humor and has the use of her other faculties. She is a law-abiding citizen who is well liked and loved. Mrs. Simmons is a human being, a person with a disability, and one who loves God. My mother is an individual who is happy and content with her relationship with God.

"To my sisters, brother, and me, she is our mother. We never looked upon her as a person with a disability. We have always looked at her as a human being who is strong and a great role model for her four children. Her weakness became her strength. Her strength, tenacity, and faith in God empowered us to be all that God intended us to be, regardless of our circumstances in life. Her disability will never define who she is as a person, and neither will it describe her true identity. My mother's name is not Crippled, Handicapped, Deformed, or even Different. Her name is Mrs. Osceola Simmons. To us, she is Mommy or Mom. She is our mother and a great woman!" My mother was a blessing to her children.

It is the name, not the disability that matters. We should not get caught up in identifying people by their disabilities; we should identify them by their names. Though all names are important to remember, there is one name in particular we should never forget: the name above all names, Jesus Christ. The apostle Paul tells us in Philippians 2:9–11 that we need to keep our minds on the name of Jesus.

> Therefore God exalted him to the highest place and gave him the name that is above every name, that at the name of Jesus every knee should bow, in heaven and on earth and under the earth, and every tongue confess that Jesus Christ is Lord, to the glory of God the Father. (NIV)

We need to remember the name of Jesus, because Luke tells us, "For the Son of Man came to seek and to save the lost" (Luke 19:10 NIV).

He can heal all our diseases and save us from our sins. Matthew reminds us in Matthew 20:28 that "the Son of Man did not come to be served, but to serve, and to give his life as a ransom for many" (NIV).

He came to die for a sinful humanity on an old, rugged cross; be buried in a borrowed tomb; and rise from the dead on the third day after His death for our justification. Jesus came to bridge the gap between God and man. Jesus came to save sinners. He came to make a way for us to be reconciled back to God, the Father. Paul tells us the following in Titus 3:5–8 and Colossians 1:19–20, respectively:

He saved us, not because of righteous things we had done, but because of his mercy. He saved us through the washing of rebirth and renewal by the Holy Spirit, whom he poured out on us generously through Jesus Christ our Savior, so that, having been justified by his grace, we might become heirs having the hope of eternal life. This is a trustworthy saying. And I want you to stress these things, so that those who have trusted in God may be careful to devote themselves to doing what is good. These things are excellent and profitable for everyone. (NIV)

For God was pleased to have all his fullness dwell in him, and through him to reconcile to himself all things, whether things on earth or things in heaven, by making peace through his blood, shed on the cross. (NIV)

You and I should not think that our names are overly important to the world or even to Jesus—at least not in the sense of what we think is important. What's important to Jesus is that we find salvation in Him so that our names can be written in the Lamb's Book of Life. The things important to the world's status quo are not the things that are important to God's holy and righteous standards. Christians are not like movie stars whose names are written in the tabloids or talked about in the media. We are citizens of a holy, righteous, and spiritual kingdom that is not of this world.

Paul tells us in Philippians 3:20–21 that we are citizens of the kingdom of heaven.

> But our citizenship is in heaven. And we eagerly await a Savior from there, the Lord Jesus Christ, who, by the power that enables him to bring everything under his control, will transform our lowly bodies so that they will be like his glorious body. (NIV)

Luke chapter 10 tells us that Jesus appointed seventy-two disciples and sent them two by two ahead of Him to every town and place He was about to enter. He gave them specific instructions about what they should do and why He was sending them forth. Upon returning from their divine assignment, they were overflowing with joy. They reported to Jesus all they had done and told him of their power over their enemies. They even boasted about how the spirits had submitted to them in Jesus's name (Luke 10:17). They thought they were somebody. However, the spirits had submitted not to their names but to the name of Jesus. Amid their excitement, Jesus had to humble them by telling them, "Do not rejoice that the spirits submit to you, but rejoice that your names are written in heaven" (Luke 10:20 NIV).

Our names are important to Jesus, especially when it comes to our eternal salvation. When we accept Jesus Christ as our personal Savior, He writes our names down in the Lamb's Book of Life.

Spiritual Disability: The Sin Issue

WE NEED TO BE CAREFUL how we depict people in life because every human being has a disability, one that is sometimes visible and sometimes hidden from the sight of man: a spiritual disability named sin. This sickness is not hidden from God's eyes. Many people don't want to acknowledge the fact that they are sinners in need of God's saving grace through the redemptive work of Jesus Christ. I have witnessed to many people about the glorious plan of God's salvation for mankind. When I talk about Jesus rising from the dead, many people reject this truth and start backing away from our conversation. Some people say things like "Nobody dies and rises again from the dead. Once we die, it is all over." They believe Jesus suffered and died but do not believe He rose from the dead three days after His death. A vital part of the Christian faith is belief in the resurrection of Jesus Christ. Romans 10:9 says, "If you declare with your mouth, 'Jesus is Lord,' and believe in your heart that God raised him from the dead, you will be saved" (NIV).

The Sadducees, religious leaders who dominated the higher echelons of the priesthood in biblical days, did not believe in the resurrection of the body, nor did they believe in angels. Their beliefs were based on the first five books of the Bible, the Pentateuch. They did not accept the psalms, prophets, or historical books of the Old Testament. Most of the Jews at that time considered these writings Scripture; however, the Sadducees based their beliefs solely on the Pentateuch. Any religious argument had to come from the Pentateuch. They did not accept the authority or the canonical status of any other book in the Old Testament.

When the apostle Paul was defending his case before the Sanhedrin, which involved Pharisees and Sadducees, a dispute broke out between the Pharisees and Sadducees because the Pharisees believed in the resurrection of the body, but the Sadducees did not. This scene is recorded in Acts 23:6-8.

> Then Paul, knowing that some of them were Sadducees and the others Pharisees, called out in the Sanhedrin, "My brothers, I am a Pharisee, descended from Pharisees. I stand on trial because of the hope of the resurrection of the dead." When he said this, a dispute broke out between the Pharisees and the Sadducees, and the assembly was divided. (The Sadducees say that there is no resurrection, and that there are neither angels nor spirits, but the Pharisees believe all these things.) (NIV)

The sin issue is real. God's people need to trust His Word and accept the fact that His Word is true. It will never lie. It will never die. It will live forever. The Bible tells us in Matthew 24:35, "Heaven and earth will pass away, but my words will never pass away" (NIV).

Many people don't believe that God sees all things. Proverbs 15:3 says, "The eyes of the LORD are everywhere, keeping watch on the wicked and the good" (NIV).

God knows the intent of every heart. His Word judges the thoughts and attitudes of our hearts and minds. If the world was not sinful and corrupt, Jesus wouldn't have had to come down through forty-two generations, take on the form of a man, and go to Calvary to die for the sins of humanity. He was the perfect Lamb of God and came to take away the sins of the world and die for a sinful humanity. If the world had believed the Word of God, the world would not have been filled with sin, corruption, and destruction. But that was not the case. Jesus had to come "save his people from their sin" (Matthew 1:21 NIV).

When we read about the supernatural miracle concerning the woman who had a spirit of infirmity, or a bent-over condition, there is no indication that her suffering was due to sin, as was the case with the nameless woman whose sins were forgiven in Luke 7:36–50. In those verses, Luke records a story about a woman who lived a sinful life. When she heard Jesus was in town having dinner at one of the Pharisees' houses, she came to the house with an alabaster jar of perfume. The woman stood behind Jesus at His feet. She was crying and began to wet His feet with her tears. She wiped His feet with her hair, kissed them, and poured perfume on them. The Pharisee was upset because this woman who wiped Jesus's feet was a sinner. The Pharisee said,

"If this man were a prophet, he would know who is touching him and what kind of woman she is—that she is a sinner" (Luke 7:39 NIV).

After Jesus told the Pharisee a story about love, forgiveness, and a repentant heart, He turned to the women and said to her, "Your sins are forgiven … Your faith has saved you; go in peace" (Luke 7:48, 50 NIV).

This woman exercised her faith in Jesus. She realized she was a sinner. Perhaps she remembered the words of the prophet Isaiah: "Seek the LORD while he may be found; call on him while he is near" (Isaiah 55:6 NIV).

If we sought God's face continually, as this woman whose sins were forgiven did, we would experience God's Word in Ephesians 3:20 in a powerful way. The apostle Paul says,

> God can do anything, you know—far more than you could ever imagine or guess or request in your wildest dreams! He does it not by pushing us around but by working within us, his Spirit deeply and gently within us. (MSG)

God's power is always at work in us, just as it was at work in the woman whose situation appears in Luke 7:36–50. This humble woman knew she had a sin issue and needed to be forgiven. She also was persistent and exercised her faith in Jesus Christ, the Great I Am. Nevertheless, the two women depicted in these stories had the same spiritual disability—sin—just as the rest of humanity does. Only one woman had to be delivered from a physical malady, but both women had to be saved and delivered from a spiritual malady: the penalty of sin, death, and eternal condemnation. These women manifested their faith in God differently and received God's saving grace.

You and I must come to grips with the sin issue. It is real, and it is deadly. The Word of God makes this clear for us in Romans 3:23 and Romans 6:23: "For all have sinned and come short of the glory of God" (KJV) and "For the wages of sin is death, but the gift of God is eternal life in Christ Jesus our Lord" (KJV).

David, a man after God's own heart, understood this clearly. He says in Psalms 51:5, "Behold, I was shapen in iniquity; and in sin did my mother conceive me" (KJV). The New Living Translation records it this way: "For I was born a sinner—yes, from the moment my mother conceived me" (NLT).

David continues by saying in Psalms 51:2, 7, 9–10,

> Wash away all my iniquity and cleanse me from my sin ... Cleanse me with hyssop, and I will be clean; wash me, and I will be whiter than snow ... Hide your face from my sins and blot out all my iniquity ... Create in me a pure heart, O God, and renew a steadfast spirit within me. (NIV)

I am the first one to admit that I am far from perfect in God's sight. I have many shortcomings that need to be removed from my life. These shortcomings are sin. There is no other name for them. Sin is sin. I shiver when I think of God's words in Matthew 5:29–30:

> If your right eye causes you to stumble, gouge it out and throw it away. It is better for you to lose one part of your body than for your whole body to be thrown into hell. And if your right hand causes you to stumble, cut it off and throw it away. It is better for you to lose one part of your body than for your whole body to go into hell. (NIV)

In the verses above, Jesus is not saying to literally gouge out your eye and throw it away. Neither is He saying to cut off your right hand and throw it away. In these verses, Jesus is using parts of the body to make an important point to all believers. He is saying that Christians should not allow habitual sins to be an integral part of their lives. Any Christian who has a sinful habit should forsake it, even if letting go of that sinful habit is as painful as losing an eye or hand. A Christian should not tolerate sin in his or her life, nor should the body of Christ tolerate sin among its members.

Personally, when I reflect on these two verses of Scripture from the lips of Jesus, I find them to be powerful, true, and profound. I do not know about you, but I would rather enter heaven with one arm or leg, one eye or ear, one kidney or foot, and a physically bent-over condition than spend eternity in hell because of habitual sin in my life. A long time ago, I decided to make Jesus my personal Lord and Savior by accepting His redemptive work for me on Calvary's cross. I keep before me the words of the apostle Paul concerning the sacrifice Jesus made for humanity: "God made him who had no sin to be sin for us, so that in him we might become the righteousness of God" (2 Corinthians 5:21 NIV).

I praise God for allowing His Son to take my sins upon Him one day on an old, rugged cross so that I could have eternal life. I needed to receive Jesus Christ as my personal Savior and Lord over my life. Why? Because like David, through the Word of God, I've come to the knowledge that I was also "born a sinner from my mother's womb—yes, from the moment my mother conceived me." I realized that I needed God to "wash away all my iniquity and cleanse me from my sin." I recognized that I needed God to "cleanse me with hyssop" so that "I will be clean; and to wash me" so that "I will be whiter than snow." I needed God to "hide his face from my sins and blot out all my iniquity" and to continuously "create in me a pure heart … and renew a steadfast spirit within me" (Psalm 51:2, 5, 7, 9–10 NIV). I still need God to help me die daily to my flesh and submit my will to His will, because I am here to do God's will (Hebrews 13:21). I need Him to unclothe me from my unrighteousness and clothe me with His righteousness. I believe the Word of God when it says, "Nothing in all creation is hidden from God's sight. Everything is uncovered and laid bare before the eyes of him to whom we must give account" (Hebrews 4:13 NIV).

God wants us to be perfect. He is not referring to moral perfection. He is talking about growing in the grace and knowledge of Jesus Christ. He wants us to live Christian lives that are holy, clean, and godly. You and I have been redeemed by the blood of the Lamb. We are not our own. We have been bought with a price. First Corinthians 6:20 clarifies this fact for us: "You were bought at a price. Therefore honor God with your body" (NIV).

If you have not been saved by Jesus Christ and His saving grace, you still have the opportunity to be sorry for your sins, repent of your sins, and ask Jesus to forgive you and save you from the penalty of sin and death. Ask Jesus to come into your heart and be your Savior and Lord. Ask Jesus to fill you with His Holy Spirit. When you join the ranks of the reborn, you inherit all the precious provisions of God. Romans 10:9–13 says,

> If you declare with your mouth, "Jesus is Lord," and believe in your heart that God raised him from the dead, you will be saved. For it is with your heart that you believe and are justified, and it is with your mouth that you profess your faith and are saved. As Scripture says, "Anyone who believes in him will never be put to shame." For there is no difference between Jew and Gentile—the same Lord is Lord of all and richly blesses all who call on

him, for, "Everyone who calls on the name of the Lord will be saved. (NIV)

The apostle Paul tells us in Romans 8:14–17 that we are adopted into the family of God. He also informs us about our spiritual inheritance in the family of God.

> For as many as are led by the Spirit of God, they are the sons of God. For ye have not received the spirit of bondage again to fear; but ye have received the Spirit of adoption, whereby we cry, Abba, Father. The Spirit itself beareth witness with our spirit, that we are the children of God: And if children, then heirs; heirs of God, and joint-heirs with Christ; if so be that we suffer with him, that we may be also glorified together. (KJV)

If we have been saved by faith in Jesus Christ, we are mandated by God's Word in Romans 12:1–2 to,

> Present your bodies as a living sacrifice, holy and pleasing to God—this is your true and proper worship. Do not conform to the pattern of this world, but be transformed by the renewing of your mind. Then you will be able to test and approve what God's will is—his good, pleasing and perfect will. (NIV)

We are children of God. We have been adopted into the family of God by the blood of Jesus Christ and are in union with Him. Therefore, we are to walk like it, look like it, talk like it, and live it. We need to praise God every day of our lives and thank Him for picking us up out of the miry clay and placing our feet on the Solid Rock of our salvation, Jesus Christ. This is the only way we can truly be righteous, serve God, honor Him, and continue having fellowship with Him. Peter tells us,

> But you are a chosen people, a royal priesthood, a holy nation, God's special possession, that you may declare the praises of him who called you out of darkness into his wonderful light" (1 Peter 2:9 NIV).

God expects us to obey Him and to "live a life worthy of the calling you have received" (Ephesians 4:1–2 NIV).

He blesses people who walk before Him with clean hands and pure hearts. God honors those who honor Him. What about you? Have you accepted Jesus Christ as your personal Savior and Lord of your life? If not, you still have the opportunity to do so and can do so this moment. The apostle Paul reminds us in Romans 10:9–11,

> That if thou shalt confess with thy mouth the Lord Jesus, and shalt believe in thine heart that God hath raised him from the dead, thou shalt be saved. For with the heart man believeth unto righteousness; and with the mouth confession is made unto salvation. For

the scripture saith, whosoever believeth on him shall not be ashamed. (KJV)

The New International Version puts it this way:

> That if you confess with your mouth, "Jesus is Lord," and believe in your heart that God raised him from the dead, you will be saved. For it is with your heart that you believe and are justified, and it is with your mouth that you confess and are saved. As the Scripture says, "Anyone who trusts in him will never be put to shame.

Yes, I know that I quoted this verse before, but I want to give you every opportunity to accept Jesus Christ as your Savior and the Lord of your life and be born again. John 3:5 says, "Except a man be born of water and of the Spirit, he cannot enter into the kingdom of God" (NIV).

God's Word promises us,

> "For all the promises of God in him are yea, and in him Amen, unto the glory of God by us" (2 Corinthians 1:20 KJV).

Adam and Eve's Disobedience: The First Sin Issue

WHEN THE LORD PLACED ADAM and Eve in the garden of Eden, He gave them a simple command in Genesis 2:16–17. He told them, "Of every tree of the garden you may freely eat; but of the tree of the knowledge of good and evil you shall not eat, for in the day that you eat of it you shall surely die" (NKJV).

As we see in Genesis chapter 3, they disobeyed God's command. God expelled them from the garden because of their sin of disobedience. Because of their sin, all of creation was cursed, including Adam's wife, Eve. God said to Eve in Genesis 3:16, "I will greatly multiply your sorrow and your conception; In pain you shall bring forth children" (NKJV).

What a curse! Eve saw the fruit, lusted after it, and ate it. The Word of God cautions us in 1 John 2:15–17,

> Do not love the world or the things in the
> world. If anyone loves the world, the love of
> the Father is not in him. For all that is in the

world—the lust of the flesh, the lust of the eyes, and the pride of life—is not of the Father but is of the world. And the world is passing away, and the lust of it; but he who does the will of God abides forever. (NKJV)

It does not pay to disobey the Word of God, because "the wages of sin is death" and not life (Romans 6:23 NIV).

The Curse

THE HORRIBLE CURSE OF PARDISE—"IN sorrow thou shall bring for children"—has a deeper meaning apart from the physical delivery of a child. It also suggests that some women will suffer in different ways even though no childbirth takes place, such as the woman with the bent-over condition in Luke 13:10–17. Yet others will suffer terribly because of the prolonged consequences of childbirth. I believe many mothers, including me, can identify with the prolonged consequences of childbearing. We say to ourselves and tell others, "I won't go through this again, because the pain is unbearable." Nevertheless, some of us find ourselves eating our words. Some of us have encountered this experience not just once, twice, or three times but six or more. The power of God's words and the consequences of sin were the same then and will remain the same until Jesus returns for His church without spot or wrinkle. God said to the woman in Genesis 3:16, "I will greatly multiply your sorrow and your conception; In pain you shall bring forth children" (NKJV). Wow! Wait until I see Eve.

However, in His own way, God does not equally divide the portion of suffering each woman is to endure. Why?

Because the quantity of suffering in each woman's cup varies; some women are made to drink only a few hasty drops of it. For others, the cup has been filled to the brim until it overflows. The woman with the bent-over condition, had a cup of suffering that overflowed from the brim into her saucer for eighteen long years. She was not the only woman who experienced a disability in the Bible. The woman with the issue of blood suffered with a disability for twelve years. She also had a bent-over condition and needed to be healed by Jesus. She believed in Jesus's ability to heal her and, by faith, came up behind Him and touched the edge of his cloak. She said to herself, "If I only touch his cloak, I will be healed" (Matthew 9:21 NIV), and she was healed. No one had been able to heal these two women of their disabilities other than Jesus. I have good news for women today: there is always hope for all, no matter how many sips a woman must drink from the cup of suffering. That hope is belief and relief in knowing that deliverance is on the way. Psalm 3:8 tells us, "From the LORD comes deliverance" (NIV).

The writer of the book of Hebrews reminds us that when we are experiencing any kind of suffering, no matter how small or great, that we have a High Priest:

> For we do not have a High Priest who cannot sympathize with our weaknesses, but was in all points tempted as we are, yet without sin. Let us therefore come boldly to the throne of grace that we may obtain mercy and find grace to help in time of need. (Hebrews 4:15–16 NKJV)

What Is Your Disability?

WHAT IS YOUR NOTICEABLE OR unnoticeable disability or bent-over condition? Is it a physical disability? Is it a spiritual disability? Is it lying? Is it envy? Is it malice? Is it jealousy? Is it sexual immorality? Is it impurity or corruption? Is it idolatry? Is it witchcraft? Is it hatred? Is it discord? Do you have fits of rage? Is it selfish ambition? Do you struggle with dissensions or factions? Is it drunkenness or participation in orgies? (Galatians 5:19–21). Whatever it is, you have a spiritual disability. You have a spiritual illness. You have a spiritual malady. It's a sin issue. Have you allowed Jesus to heal you from your sin issue? If not, you can still come in direct contact with Jesus, just as I did many years ago. I remember Jesus's words in John 6:37 clearly: "All that those the Father gives me will come to me, and whoever comes to me I will never drive away" (NIV).

I thank Jesus for His saving grace and for not driving me away from Him because of my sins.

Charlotte Elliott

IN READING THE SHORT BIOGRAPHY of Charlotte Elliott in a book entitled *101 Hymn Stories*, I learned that she had a disability. Charlotte was born in Clapham, England, on March 18, 1789. As a young person, she lived a carefree life, gaining popularity as a portrait artist and writer of humorous verses. By the time she was thirty, however, her health began to fail rapidly, and soon she became a bedridden woman. Charlotte lived with her disability, or bent-over condition, for the rest of her life. With her failing health came a great feeling of despondency.[24] At some point in her life, she remembered the words of Jesus in John 6:35, 37:

> Then Jesus declared, "I am the bread of life. Whoever comes to me will never go hungry, and whoever believes in me will never be thirsty ... All those the Father gives me will

[24] Osbeck, Kenneth W., *101 Hymn Stories* (Grand Rapids, Michigan: Kregel Publications, 1986), 146.

come to me, and whoever comes to me I will never drive away." (NIV)

From this verse of Scripture, she authored the hymn *Just as I Am*. Her disability did not hinder her mind; it only afflicted her body. Think about this hymn with every ounce of your soul as you read it, and let it speak to your heart. The last verse is a promise to everyone who has not received Jesus Christ as his or her Savior.

Just as I Am

Just as I am, without one plea,
But that thy blood was shed for me,
And that Thou bidst me come to Thee
Oh Lamb of God, I come! I come!

Just as I am, Thou wilt receive,
Wilt welcome, pardon, cleanse, relieve,
Be-cause Thy promise I believe,
Oh Lamb of God, I come! I come![25]

As Kenneth Osbeck says in *101 Hymn Stories,* "Without question, this hymn has touched more hearts and influenced more people for Christ than any other song ever written. The text was born within the soul of a woman who had a disability. This song came from a woman who wrote these words out of intense feeling of uselessness and despair."[26]

---

[25] Ibid.
[26] Ibid.

Some people in our society today would call her an invalid instead of viewing her as a woman with a sharp mind.

For this reason, it pleases me to notice that the gospel also includes comfort for those who suffer in various ways. It tells us how a woman who suffered from a disability that made her "bowed together" into a bent-over condition came in direct contact with Jesus.

When it comes to the four Gospels, each writer addresses a particular group of people. Matthew places emphasis on Jesus as the promised Messiah foretold in the Old Testament. His writings were for the Jews. Mark writes about the superhuman power of Jesus Christ and demonstrates the deity of Jesus by telling of His miracles. He targeted the Romans with his writing. When Luke, known as the beloved physician, wrote his gospel, he focused on Jesus's humanity, kindness toward the weak, and suffering and on the outcast in society. Luke had the Greeks in mind when he wrote his gospel. John's writings place special emphasis on the deity of Jesus Christ, and he wrote them with all men in mind. Each writer penned his words according to his own unique characteristics and style.

Luke

LUKE, WHO WAS A TRAINED physician, observer, and gifted historian, was in a better position than the other gospel writers to tell us about the infinite healing power Jesus possessed. He was in the position of diagnosing an individual's physical condition and could state according to his findings whether the individual was going to recover from his or her sickness or was in the process of facing death. Luke does not do this in his gospel. He focuses on the works of Jesus and not upon himself. Luke writes about some of the miracles Jesus performed without any justification. He presents a simple record of the miracles of Jesus as they happened. In the case of Jesus healing a leper, Luke does not talk about the disease of leprosy or tell how Jesus might have produced the healing. In the story of Jesus healing a mute man who could not speak, Luke does not give a reason to explain why the man could not talk. He also does not give an explanation concerning why the woman with the issue of blood could not be cured. The disease of leprosy was real; in reality, the mute man could not speak; and the woman with the issue of blood spent all her money on doctors but was never cured. Luke does not analyze these problems or explain them or describe them in detail. He wanted people to know the miracles of Jesus, as they demonstrated His power and authority. As a disciple of Jesus Christ and a trained physician, Luke came to realize that there was a physician greater than he: Jesus Christ. His aim was to encourage people to trust in Jesus's miraculous power and the divine authority bestowed upon Him by His Father.

The Synagogue

THIS PARTICULAR MIRACLE, WHICH HAPPENED in one of the synagogues on the Jewish Sabbath, is documented in Luke 13:10: "On a Sabbath Jesus was teaching in one of the synagogues" (NIV).

Attending the synagogue was not unusual for Jesus. It was His custom to go to the synagogue on the Sabbath (Luke 4:16). On the other hand, it was not His custom to perform a miracle on the Sabbath or in a synagogue.

The Bible records at least thirty-five to forty miracles Jesus performed during His earthly ministry. Out of these miracles, He only executed seven miracles on the Sabbath. He performed four of His acts of mercy and grace on the Sabbath in different places, and three miracles happened in the synagogue. The miracle of the woman bowed over, or the woman with a spirit of infirmity, in Luke's narrative happened not only on the Sabbath but also in the synagogue.

Luke recorded in his gospel that the religious leaders were always watching Jesus closely so that they could find ways of trapping Him in wrongdoing on the Sabbath. He tells us the following in Luke 6:7 and Luke 14:1, respectively:

"So the scribes and Pharisees watched Him closely, whether He would heal on the Sabbath, that they might find an accusation against Him" (NKJV) and "Now it happened, as He went into the house of one of the rulers of the Pharisees to eat bread on the Sabbath, that they watched Him closely" (NKJV).

In other words, the religious leaders wanted to get rid of Jesus because He had become popular among the people. The Word of God says Jesus went about preaching the good news of the gospel. Mark documents this in Mark 1:15: "'The time has come,' he said. 'The kingdom of God has come near. Repent and believe the good news'" (NIV).

Jesus proclaimed to be the representative of His Father in John 8:42:

"If God were your Father, you would love me, for I have come here from God. I have not come on my own; God sent me" (NIV). The religious leaders felt threatened by Jesus because of His influence on the people. They believed Jesus was taking the attention of the people away from them and their teaching and was causing the people to focus on Him and His teaching. They were envious, jealous, resentful, intimidated, and afraid of Jesus' authority and power.

The same kind of behavior exists in our society today among some of our leaders and our brothers and sisters. Some leaders in our Christian family are envious, jealous, resentful, and intimidated by other colleagues for one reason or another. Some leaders are jealous over someone else's ministry. Others are intimidated by another colleague's preaching style or another preacher's humble spirit. Some Christian leaders are envious because they believe God endowed another with more power than they possess. When the Spirit of God encourages a person to move his or her membership from one church to another, some pastors say that another pastor is stealing their members. Some leaders are focused on another leader's ministry and what he or she is doing instead of fulfilling the ministry to which God has called them. Nevertheless, there are thousands and thousands of leaders whose focus is completely on serving God and His people with genuine hearts.

Yes, we have a lot of crazy stuff going on in the family of God, just as we did in biblical days. Somebody is always seeking to trap or find fault with another's ministry rather than focusing on his or her own divine assignment. Many people who are seeking healing, salvation, deliverance, wholeness, and a word from the Lord are being robbed because of Christian leaders who have taken their eyes off of Jesus, the Author and Finisher of our faith. This is what was happening in the synagogue; the religious leaders attended the synagogue with wrong motives. They wanted to find fault with Jesus so that they could get rid of Him.

We know healing on the Sabbath was one of the issues the ruler had against Jesus, but it seems that the place where Jesus performed this miraculous act also was problematic for the ruler. Why? Because the miracle happened in the synagogue (Luke 13:10). The Scripture says, "On the Sabbath Jesus was teaching in one of the synagogues" (NIV).

Why the focus on the synagogue? In fact, what is a synagogue, and what is its significance? What did the synagogue represent to the Jews and their religious leaders?

The Importance and Purpose of the Synagogue

IF YOU RESEARCH THE WORD *synagogue*, you'll discover that it means a gathering of people, a congregation, a Jewish religious community, or a sanctuary. The synagogue in the story was a little sanctuary where people who lived nearby gathered for worship and instruction.[27]

When Israel was taken into captivity and placed in a foreign land, God appeared to Ezekiel in a vision and instructed him to speak to Israel as follows:

> Therefore say: "This is what the Sovereign LORD says: Although I sent them far away among the nations and scattered them among the countries, yet for a little while I have been a sanctuary for them in the countries where they have gone." (Ezekiel 11:16 NIV)

---

[27] Madeleine S. Miller and J. Lane Miller, *Synagogues and Rulers* (New York: Harper and Row 1973), 717.

The synagogue was a place where both adults and children learned the law and received instruction concerning God's will for their lives.[28] The Israelites were to obey the instructions they received throughout their daily lives, not just on the Sabbath. The synagogue was also used as a social center where community problems were discussed and solved, legal transactions of interest to the congregation were posted, and funerals were held and alms received.[29] The synagogue has been called "the spiritual home of the Jews," and the synagogue was a place of trial and punishment.[30] Jesus said to His disciples in Matthew 10:17, "Be on your guard; you will be handed over to the local councils and be flogged in the synagogues" (NIV).

The woman who'd suffered from a bent-over condition for eighteen years was in the right place, because a synagogue was—and still is—a place where the Jews would congregate together, especially on the Jewish Sabbath, to offer prayers to God, witness, and expound on the Old Testament Scriptures. Luke 4:16–21 gives us an example of how Jesus expounded on the Old Testament when He went to the synagogue on the Sabbath.

> He went to Nazareth, where he had been brought up, and on the Sabbath day he went into the synagogue, as was his custom. He stood up to read, and the scroll of the prophet Isaiah was handed to him. Unrolling it, he

---

[28] Ibid.

[29] Ibid.

[30] Ibid. 718.

found the place where it is written, The Spirit
of the Lord is on me, because he has anointed
me to proclaim good news to the poor. He has
sent me to proclaim freedom for the prisoners
and recovery of sight for the blind, to set the
oppressed free, to proclaim the year of the
Lord's favor. Then he rolled up the scroll, gave
it back to the attendant and sat down. The eyes
of everyone in the synagogue were fastened on
him. He began by saying to them, "Today this
scripture is fulfilled in your hearing." (NIV)

Here we find our Lord and Savior quoting verses of
Scripture taken from the Old Testament in Isaiah 61:1–2.
This is not the first time Jesus quotes Scriptures from the
Old Testament. He quotes Scripture from Deuteronomy 6:5
and Leviticus 19:18b.

On the Sabbath, morning worship services were held in
the synagogue. Sometimes evening worship services were
also held on the same day. In the majority of the synagogues,
morning worship services in the beginning of the Christian
era started with psalms, benedictions, and the Shema, the
Jewish Creed. This was followed by reciting the Amidah,
a prayer made up of eighteen benedictions, followed by
the Jewish Creed. Next came a sermon or interpretation by
any member of the synagogue or by a guest, as recorded in
Luke 4:16.[31] Scripture tells us that when Jesus attended the
synagogue on the Sabbath, "he went to Nazareth, where he

---

[31] Ibid.

had been brought up, and on the Sabbath day he went into the synagogue, as was his custom. And he stood up to read" (Luke 4:16 NIV).

On certain days, portions of the law and words of the prophets were read. Then the head or ruler of the synagogue pronounced a blessing that engaged the congregation in praise. The ruler of the synagogue would then close out the service with the Aaronic blessing recorded in Numbers 6:24–26: "The LORD bless you and keep you; the LORD make his face shine upon you and be gracious to you; the LORD turn his face toward you and give you peace" (NIV).

The atmosphere was joyous and reminiscent, as the assembly faced in the direction of the Jerusalem Temple E for most of the Diaspora.[32]

The synagogue is closely related to the church. Jesus learned and taught in the local synagogue at Nazareth. He even prophesied about what would happen to His followers in times to come regarding the synagogue.[33] He said in John 16:2, "They will put you out of the synagogue; in fact, the time is coming when anyone who kills you will think they are offering a service to God" (NIV).

His first followers continued to worship in the Jerusalem Temple for a time (Acts 3:11). They also used the synagogues as teaching places and centers for gathering new recruits, as Paul did in Corinth, Cyprus, Antioch and practically every city he entered.[34] The Word of God says, "Just as Paul was about to speak, Gallio said to them, 'If you Jews were

---

[32] Ibid.
[33] Ibid.
[34] Ibid.

making a complaint about some misdemeanor or serious crime, it would be reasonable for me to listen to you'" (Acts 18:14 NIV), and "When they arrived at Salamis, they proclaimed the word of God in the Jewish synagogues. John was with them as their helper" (Acts 13:5 NIV).

The apostle Paul recruited Gentiles adherent, or fearers of God, from the synagogue, as in Acts 10:2. Such individuals had accepted the moral teaching of Judaism but had not become full adherents through circumcision. Acts tells us, "He and all his family were devout and God-fearing; he gave generously to those in need and prayed to God regularly" (NIV).

The church took over its Scripture reading, praying, and preaching from the synagogue. The synagogue gave the church more than any other Jewish institution did.[35] It is important to understand that the synagogue is a vital part in the lives of Jews, just as the church plays an important role in the lives of Christians.

---

[35] Ibid. 629–630, 717–718.

Rulers

THE BIBLE SPEAKS ABOUT RULERS and the different types of positions they held. A ruler is a person who governs with authority or is head of a group. Genesis 47:6 calls herdsmen "rulers over cattle." Exodus 18:25 tells us how Moses appointed rulers during his era. He called them chieftains, and they were rulers or officials over anywhere from tens to thousands. During the period of Judges, Jephthah was ruler, or judge, over Gilead (Judges 11:8). King David was the "ruler over Israel," as recorded in 1 Samuel 25:30. The directors he appointed over public works were rulers of special projects, as stated in 1 Chronicles 29:6. Persian satraps were rulers over provinces during Esther's time, as noted in Esther 8:9. In the New Testament, Luke tells us that a governor or king was called a ruler. Acts 16:19 refers to the local Greek magistrates as rulers.

In fact, throughout the entire Bible, God is regarded as the Ruler of the kingdom of men, as recorded in Judges 8:23: "But Gideon told them, 'I will not rule over you, nor will my son rule over you. The LORD will rule over you'" (NIV).

The head of the synagogue was its ruler. Jairus and Crispus were rulers of the synagogue. The following verses of Scripture support this fact.

> And the land of Egypt is before you; settle your father and your brothers in the best part of the land. Let them live in Goshen. And if you know of any among them with special ability, put them in charge of my own livestock. (Genesis 47:6 NIV)

> He chose capable men from all Israel and made them leaders of the people, officials over thousands, hundreds, fifties and tens. (Exodus 18:2 NIV)

> Then one of the synagogue leaders, named Jairus, came, and when he saw Jesus, he fell at his feet. (Mark 5:22 NIV)

> Crispus, the synagogue leader, and his entire household believed in the Lord; and many of the Corinthians who heard Paul believed and were baptized. (Acts 18:8 NIV)

The ruler was in charge of worship services and selected the men who led prayer, read from the Torah, and preached.[36] An example of this is located in Acts 13:14–15, when Paul went to Pisidian Antioch. The Word of God says,

---

[36] Ibid. 717.

> On the Sabbath they entered the synagogue
> and sat down. After the reading from the Law
> and the Prophets, the leaders of the synagogue
> sent word to them, saying, "Brothers, if you
> have a word of exhortation for the people,
> please speak." (NIV)

Sometimes the office of ruler was hereditary. It exacted so much time that in the Roman period, the synagogue ruler was exempt from his usual public duties.[37] A ruler is always an important individual because he or she governs with authority. In the narrative recorded in Luke 13:14, Jesus encountered an unpleasant experience with the ruler of the synagogue, because Jesus had healed the woman on the Sabbath. Luke tells us how the ruler reacted when he watched what Jesus did in the life of this woman who'd had a terrible malady for eighteen years.

---

[37] Ibid.

The Ruler: A Worshipper with a Hidden Agenda

THE RULER IN LUKE'S NARRATIVE, failed to realize that he had a zeal for God, but not according to knowledge (Romans 10:2). Therefore, Jesus called the ruler a hypocrite. A hypocrite is a person who pretends to be what he or she is not. Jesus condemned the ruler's behavior because the ruler was assuming a persona. The ruler conscientiously observed the law and its rites and ceremonies. He was jealous of Jesus splendor and superiority, because he believed the law came from God. Therefore, he sinned more out of ignorance than spite. The ruler was angry because Jesus had gone against the way he thought the service was supposed to be carried out. Since the preaching, prayer meeting, convictions, and conversions were not carried out his way, he felt, the service was not of God. He wasn't concerned about the woman's well-being or healing. He would rather have taken his ox to get a drink of water than seen Jesus carry out another one of His acts of mercy.

The ruler had a spirit of indignation and lacked a heart of compassion. The words Jesus spoke to the ruler caused the ruler to take off his mask of hypocrisy. The ruler's merciless heart not only turned against Jesus but also became an instrument in edifying the people attending the service in the synagogue. The people recognized how hypocritical the ruler's heart was and praised God for the wonderful things Jesus had done in the woman's life.

Both the woman and the ruler had the right to be in the synagogue on the Sabbath, but their motives for being there were different. The woman came to hear a word from the Lord and to worship God in spirit and truth. The ruler came to observe Jesus to see if he could catch Him breaking the Jewish law on the Sabbath.

It was mainly on the Sabbath when the Pharisees, religious leaders of the Jewish community, would enter the synagogues and pray in their religious pride and self-righteousness. They were zealous observers of religious rules and maintained outward appearances of righteous conduct. They believed they were uniquely qualified to be accepted by God when they came to the synagogue to pray. They would inform God about their own goodness and righteousness. Luke recorded a story about a Pharisee and a publican in Luke 18:9–14 in order to caution us against exalting ourselves.

> To some who were confident of their own righteousness and looked down on everybody else, Jesus told this parable: "Two men went up to the temple to pray, one a Pharisee and the other a tax collector. The Pharisee stood up and prayed about himself: 'God, I thank

you that I am not like other men—robbers, evildoers, adulterers—or even like this tax collector. I fast twice a week and give a tenth of all I get.' But the tax collector stood at a distance. He would not even look up to heaven, but beat his breast and said, 'God, have mercy on me, a sinner.' I tell you that this man, rather than the other, went home justified before God. For everyone who exalts himself will be humbled, and he who humbles himself will be exalted." (NIV)

This story portrays the truth of how we should go before God when we pray to Him. God honors a humble and contrite heart like the publican's and not one full of pride like the Pharisee's. God will bring down the proud and exalt the humble. A humble and contrite spirit qualifies a praying person to receive all kinds of answers and blessings from the Lord.

The Pharisees prayed, and the synagogue was the place for prayer and instruction, just as the Christian church is today. Church is a place to hear the Word of God, pray, receive instruction, witness, and worship God in spirit and in truth. But as with the ruler who entered the synagogue with sinful motives, some Christians enter the church today with impure motives. The ruler had a hidden agenda, as do some Christians on any given Sunday when they come into the house of the Lord. Their intentions are to watch what others are doing so that they can find fault with them instead of lifting up holy hands unto the Lord and worshipping

God. It seems some find it easier, when in the Lord's house, to focus on other people and find fault with them instead of focusing on themselves. I know this is true because I have done so myself. There have been times when the preacher was praying, but instead of bowing my head, closing my eyes, and focusing on the Lord and prayer, I was looking around to see what others were doing. If we don't focus on ourselves when we are in the house of God, then we are not allowing God to help us deal with our own personal issues. We are quick to judge other people for their actions. Jesus spoke about the issue of judging others in terms of looking for the specks in our sisters' and brothers' eyes when we have planks in our own eyes. In Jesus's discourse on the Sermon on the Mount, He said in Matthew 7:1–5,

> Do not judge, or you too will be judged. For in the same way you judge others, you will be judged, and with the measure you use, it will be measured to you. Why do you look at the speck of sawdust in your brother's eye and pay no attention to the plank in your own eye? How can you say to your brother, "Let me take the speck out of your eye," when all the time there is a plank in your own eye? You hypocrite, first take the plank out of your own eye, and then you will see clearly to remove the speck from your brother's eye. (NIV)

This was the ruler's intention when he went into the synagogue—judging others. He watched Jesus as closely as he could, hoping to catch him breaking the Jewish law concerning the Sabbath. He criticized Jesus for healing a woman with a bent-over condition on the Sabbath. After watching Jesus perform this miracle, he thought he had caught Jesus breaking the law on the Sabbath; however, Jesus is the Lord of the Sabbath, not us.

The Lord of the Sabbath

IN THIS NARRATIVE, THE RULER, as religious as he was, did not recognize who was the Lord of the Sabbath. It certainly wasn't him in his righteous pride. The ruler did not understand, in his unbelief in the One who knows the heart of every human being and can read the thoughts of a man even before they enter his mind, that he was condemning the One who gave the law from the fiery mount. Jesus is part of the triune Godhead. Jehovah told Moses to tell His people that the Great I Am said,

> Remember the Sabbath day by keeping it holy. Six days you shall labor and do all your work, but the seventh day is a sabbath to the LORD your God. On it you shall not do any work, neither you, nor your son or daughter, nor your male or female servant, nor your animals, nor any foreigner residing in your towns. For in six days the LORD made the heavens and the earth, the sea, and all that is in them, but he rested on the seventh day. Therefore the LORD

blessed the Sabbath day and made it holy.
(Exodus 20:8–11 NIV)

How many times have we disobeyed the Word of God on the Sabbath? Some of us who claim to be born again of the Holy Spirit don't even go to church on the Lord's Day. We stay home and clean our houses, wash our cars, go to the movies, go grocery shopping, and even play all sorts of sports on Sundays. We do these chores not out of necessity but because we choose not to honor the Lord's Day. If these were works of necessity, that would be a different issue. God's instructions did not say that God could not work but that "man should not work." We must remember Mark 2:27, which says, "The Sabbath was made for man and not man for the Sabbath. Therefore the Son of Man is Lord also of the Sabbath" (KJV).

Jesus is one with the Father and Holy Spirit. He was always included in the affairs and ways of His Father. Genesis 1:1 says, "In the beginning God created the heavens and the earth." John confirms this fact for us in the New Testament: "In the beginning was the Word, and the Word was with God, and the Word was God" (John 1:1 NIV).

Jesus confirmed his involvement when he said in Mark 2:27, "The Sabbath was made for man, and not man for the Sabbath" (NIV).

Jesus was and is always involved in the affairs of His Father and men. He is eternal. He is infinite. In Hebrews 13:8, we read that "Jesus Christ is the same yesterday and today and forever" (NIV). He was, is, and always will be. The psalmist tells us in Psalm 90:2, "Before the mountains were born or you brought forth the earth and the world, from everlasting to everlasting you are God" (NIV). Jesus is from everlasting to everlasting.

In reprimanding the ruler, Jesus was saying that He was master of the Sabbath, was greater than the Sabbath, and could do whatever acts of mercy or necessity needed to be done, even on the Sabbath. The daughter of Abraham's miracle was an act of mercy and necessity. She had been in a bent-over condition for eighteen long years. The Pharisee's sin was heightened by the fact that he was supposed to be a religious leader of God's chosen people; instead, he was a hypocrite, as Jesus pointed out in Luke 13:15.

A Daughter of Abraham

HAVE YOU EVER ENCOUNTERED A person suffering from a disability? Perhaps it was a relative, a person in the grocery store, someone in the workplace, or someone on a bus, in the doctor's office, or in some other public place. Whether or not you knew the person personally, if you have come across this kind of experience, then perhaps you can picture this physically challenged, "bowed together" woman walking or standing before you. It amazes me that this woman did not allow her malady to prevent her from attending the synagogue on the Sabbath day. She was a worshipper who worshiped Jehovah in and out of season. It did not matter if she had good days or bad days; she worshipped the Lord in spirit and truth. As I stated earlier, she did not have a name in the story; instead, she was called a daughter of Abraham, and she was more precious in the eyes of Jesus than the ox or ass about which He chided the Pharisees. The title by which Jesus called her perhaps suggests she was one of the inner circle of the pious Israelites. Like Simeon waiting for the consolation of Israel, she was waiting for the promised Messiah to arrive in town. Just as Zacchaeus was a son of Abraham, likewise, this woman was a daughter of Abraham. She was an inheritress of Abraham and had a firm belief in Jehovah. This nameless woman, unlike many of us today, was being inwardly moved by the Spirit of God to go to the synagogue on the Sabbath day.

This woman's physical disability probably made walking difficult for her, because the story says she was "bowed together," or, in simpler terms, was in a bent-over position. Luke says, "She was bent over and could not straighten up at all" (Luke 13:11 NIV).

Luke does not tell us how bent over the woman was, but it sounds as if she could not fully straighten herself up to see where she was going as she traveled to the house of worship. I don't know how she arrived at the synagogue on the Sabbath. There is no indication that someone walked with her to the synagogue, nor is there any suggestion that someone brought her there on a donkey or in a chariot. Luke only tells us she was in the synagogue on the Sabbath when Jesus was teaching. I like to believe she must have been familiar enough with the pattern in the road to find her way to the synagogue. However, what amazes me is not how she arrived at the synagogue but that her seat was never vacant in the congregation on the Sabbath.

When I tried picturing in my mind this daughter of Abraham walking to the synagogue, the image made me reflect on my mother's disability. I thought about how physically challenging it must have been for my mother to walk from one place to another, especially when she had to go to work. My mother's disability was not due to some kind of mysterious derangement of the nervous system.

Her malady was a result of developing polio as a child, a disease that gave her problems with both of her legs. She had a terrible limp when she walked, which made walking difficult for her until she could not walk anymore. Going up and down the stairs was always a great challenge for her. She had to make sure she watched every step she took, because if she didn't, she would easily stumble and fall. I always admired my mother—and will for the rest of my life—because she let nothing prevent her from walking from one place to the next for as long as she could. Her determination to walk when she could was strong, regardless of how long it took her to walk from one place to another.

When I was around nine years old, my mother took me to Radio City Music Hall to see a live stage show. I remember her taking my hand and holding it as we crossed the street. I said, "Mommy, I don't need you to hold my hand. I'm a big girl. I can walk by myself."

My mother responded, "I know you are a big girl, but if I fall down, you are going to fall down with me." Well, I didn't think that was funny at all. I didn't want to fall any more than she did. I didn't want her to hurt herself, and I definitely did not want to hurt myself. Well, praise God—neither one of us fell. We made it across the street safely.

This woman in Luke chapter 13 reminds me of my mother. She was determined to live regardless of her bent-over condition. She had an infirmity, but her sickness did not stop her from continuously seeking comfort for her inner spirit. I believe within my spirit that she kept repeating over and over again in her mind, If *I keep my spirit intact and keep a right relationship with God, I can cope with my illness.*

The Woman's Diagnosis

LUKE DESCRIBES THIS WOMAN TO us as pitiable. For eighteen long years, she had endured this deformity known as "a spirit of infirmity." This daughter of Abraham had a mysterious derangement of the nervous system, with origins in the mind rather than in the body. In other words, her sickness was partly physical and partly mental. The Scripture tells us in Luke 13:11 that "she was bent over; and could not straighten up at all." The phrase "bent over" is found nowhere else in the New Testament; this phrase indicates a dislocation of the vertebrae of the spine. Eighteen years is a long time to be in a condition that causes a great deal of stress to a person physically, mentally, and spiritually. Remember, her condition was partly physical and partly mental.

In this woman's case, Satan seemed to have the power of mental suggestion, which eventually manifested physically. Only the Word and Spirit of God could halt and hinder this demon, and she expressed belief in this by her words and actions. The infirmity caused her a great deal of pain and despair. With this type of condition, she must have felt depressed, despondent, powerless, and hopeless at times over the course of those eighteen years, even though the text does not tell us this was the case. She probably wondered if she would ever get well.

A lot of people fall apart when they are sick for only one week, because they don't know how to handle their maladies or how to cope with pain. I am talking about illnesses more serious than common colds, headaches, or stomachaches. Some people's maladies and suffering cause them to be mean to everyone they encounter. This is understandable. If you have ever been seriously ill, then you will relate to the fact that severe suffering is not easy to handle. It alters a person's attitude and spirit, especially if the pain or suffering seems like as if it has no end. Think about how you handle pain for any length of time, whether for a day, a week, a month, or years. Are you always pleasant to everyone you encounter when you are physically ill? Have there been times when you've wanted to just snap someone's head off? What is your spiritual attitude like when you suffer with a serious illness? Are you praising God in the midst of your situation, or are you asking God the following, as many of us do when we are on our beds of affliction: "Lord, why me? I serve you, pay tithes, go to prayer meeting, and even attend Sunday school. Lord, why me?" Instead of asking "Lord, why me?" perhaps we need to be praising God and praying for His divine healing. Maybe thinking about our own suffering will give us some insight when we are around people who are suffering from serious illnesses. We must realize that no two individuals handle sickness or pain in the same way, no matter how severe the pain is.

I used to say to people that I could handle pain well, until one day, when I had a serious accident. That accident changed my life and altered my spirit and mind. The accident occurred in 2003, and I am still suffering from it this present day. Once I changed my attitude about my pain and physical limitations, I was able to cope with my malady, and I started experiencing healing from the divine hands of God. It took me three years to accept the malady, but praise be to God that I am mending slowly. Our attitudes and fellowship with God can help us overcome any trial we encounter in life.

Put yourself in this woman's place for a moment, and ask yourself the following questions: If that had been me, how would I have mentally handled this kind of illness? Would I have felt depressed? Would I have felt powerless, as if there were no hope for me? Would I have felt despondent and hopeless about healing and life itself?

Well, if you have ever experienced any kind of sickness over a period of three weeks to a month, then I'm sure your answer to nearly every question was yes. Such illnesses also bring many complaints day after day, hour after hour, and moment after moment. Why? Because when things are not going well in our lives, we sometimes display another side of us to others. The ugly and complaining side of us pops up from somewhere and manifests itself. This side can show for reasons other than sickness as well—a financial issue, a nasty divorce, the loss of a job, or a child using drugs. These issues all test our endurance and faith. Any type of unpleasant situation you encounter in your life can cause this reaction.

We are emotional beings. God designed us that way. He gave all males and females emotions, or feelings. At some point in our lives, we experience and manifest all kinds of feelings, including anger, rejection, abandonment, powerlessness, frustration, loneliness, helplessness, and hopelessness. I am sure the bent-over woman wrestled with some of these emotions. The story doesn't tell us what kind of process she went through for eighteen years in dealing with her condition. God uses our feelings to shape us according to His divine will and purpose. The apostle Paul tells us in 1 Corinthians 6:19–20, "You are not your own; you were bought at a price" (NIV).

The Infirmity of Sin

SOME PEOPLE ARE FREE OF physical infirmities, but no one is free of the infirmity of sin. Sin is a sickness and can make us demonstrate behaviors that are demeaning, degrading, and destructive. The sad thing about sin is that the majority of the time, we fail to recognize how many people our sins hurt and affect. Our sins always hurt, touch, or influence the lives of other people.

Some people think that because they are saved by the blood and power of Jesus Christ, they are free from sinning while living on this earth. They fail to digest the words of the apostle Paul in Romans 3:23: "For all have sinned and fall short of the glory of God" (NIV).

This verse of Scripture includes saved and unsaved people. Each one of us was born in sin and shaped in iniquity. Being saved by Jesus Christ does not mean that the natural man, our fleshly nature, is no longer present in us. We are always going to wrestle with the two natures living within us, the flesh and the spirit. The flesh wants to love the world and all that is in it, including the cravings of our flesh, the lust of our eyes, and boasts about what we have that does not come from the Father but from the world (1 John 2:15–16 NIV). This war is going to continue in us until Jesus comes back for His church without spot or wrinkle. It does not matter how saved, holy, good, or righteous we think we are; every human being has sinned and comes short of the glory of God. Paul documents this truth in Romans 7:14–25.

> We know that the law is spiritual; but I am unspiritual, sold as a slave to sin. I do not understand what I do. For what I want to do I do not do, but what I hate I do. And if I do what I do not want to do, I agree that the law is good. As it is, it is no longer I myself who do it, but it is sin living in me. I know that nothing good lives in me, that is, in my sinful nature. For I have the desire to do what is good, but I cannot carry it out. For what I do is not the good I want to do; no, the evil I do not want to do—this I keep on doing. Now if I do what I do not want to do, it is no longer I who do it, but it is sin living in me that does it. So I find this law at work: When I want to do good, evil is right there with me. For in my inner being I delight in God's law; but I see another law at work in the members of my body, waging war against the law of my mind and making me a prisoner of the law of sin at work within my members. What a wretched man I am! Who will rescue me from this body of death?

Thanks be to God—through Jesus Christ our Lord! So then, I myself in my mind am a slave to God's law, but in the sinful nature a slave to the law of sin. (NIV).

When we allow our household chores, families, tiredness, and sports to prevent us from finding our way to the Lord's house on the Lord's Day, we are not only committing a sin but also not seeking a cure for our souls.

Our Spiritual Malady

SATAN'S AIM IS TO STRIP us of our fellowship with God by tempting us to sin. When we allow this to happen, the Devil puts us in a bent-over condition. We are unable to straighten ourselves up and look up into the face of Jesus, who has the strength to cure us of our evil plight of sin. Only Jesus has the power to deliver us from this horrible position. If you can picture this woman bent over before you, then you can see how your spiritual condition appears when you're in a sin-bowed-down condition. Once again, I am not saying that sin was the cause of this woman's affliction. The Scriptures do not tell us that this woman was bound because of sin. But just as a messenger of Satan was given to the apostle Paul to buffet him, so was this woman's malady bound by Satan. Paul said, "And lest I should be exalted above measure by the abundance of the revelations, a thorn in the flesh was given to me, a messenger of Satan to buffet me, lest I be exalted above measure" (2 Corinthians 12:7 KJV).

Luke tells us in Luke 13:16 that the daughter of Abraham had a spirit of infirmity, and in 2 Corinthians 12:7, Paul said he had a "thorn in the flesh." Both of them had infirmities, though their diagnoses were different. The word *thorn* means "splinter," "stake," or "something pointed." Have you ever gotten a splinter in your finger? If so, do you remember what it felt like? It wasn't a pleasant experience. It was painful. The deeper the splinter, the more your finger hurt. When I was a child, I was always getting splinters in my fingers from climbing trees and playing in the park with my friends. When I could not pull a splinter out of my finger, my mother would burn the tip of a needle and pick it out of my finger, a process that was more painful than having the splinter in my finger.

I am not sure I can imagine what Paul felt like with a thorn in his flesh, bothering him from time to time. I am not sure if his pain felt like a splinter, a stake, or something pointed. Whatever his pain felt like, there were times when this thorn prevented him from traveling from one place to another. Some interpret the thorn as a physical ailment, based on what the apostle Paul said in Galatians 4:13–14. Others suggest Paul had problems with his eyes, based on what he said in Galatians 4:15: "I can testify that, if you could have done so, you would have torn out your eyes and given them to me" (NIV).

Whatever Paul's thorn was, God permitted Satan to buffet him, just as He did with Job in Job chapters 1 and 2. The word *buffet* means to "strike with a fist." Paul was saying his thorn was like a strike with a fist. His thorn was a painful and humiliating experience given to him to prevent him from manifesting a spirit of pride. Perhaps he kept before him the words of Solomon in Proverbs 16:18:

"Pride goes before destruction and a haughty spirit before the fall" (NKJV).

Each one of us needs to understand that pride sees and does everything backward. It has a personality of its own. God does not receive praise or glory through our lives when we are full of pride. A spirit of pride is an abomination to God, who is the giver of every good and perfect gift. When we elevate ourselves with a spirit of pride, we face a formidable foe. God will fight against our plans, because they are not in line with His perfect will for our lives. James tells us in James 4:6, "God resists the proud, but gives grace to the humble" (NKJV).

God wants to use us as ambassadors to carry out His divine will and plans for His kingdom down here on Earth. But He wants us to stay humble before Him. When we walk humble before the Lord, He will exalt us in due time. God took Paul to a spiritual place in Him in ways he could not fathom. Perhaps this is one of the reasons Paul said in 1 Corinthians 2:9–10,

> But as it is written, Eye hath not seen, nor ear heard, neither have entered into the heart of man, the things which God hath prepared for them that love him. But God hath revealed them unto us by his Spirit: for the Spirit searcheth all things, yea, the deep things of God. (KJV)

The daughter of Abraham in Luke 13 did not manifest any signs of a spirit of pride. She not only cast all of her cares upon the Lord but also humbled herself under the mighty hands of God.

This woman with a long-lived physical disability never allowed her faith and commitment to God to waver. She never allowed her affliction to stop her from making the sacrifice of worshipping God in spirit and in truth. If she had not had faith in God, she would not have been in the right place at the right time to be cured by the healing hands of the Great Physician. Regardless of her condition, it was her habitual custom on the Lord's Day to go to the house of worship and ask, "Is there any word from the Lord so that my soul could be revived?" Her illness caused her a great deal of constant pain and mental anguish. In spite of her malady, for eighteen long years, she carried herself and her condition to the house of worship. Bent over or not, she was there in the synagogue.

Sometimes the permissive will of God touches our lives. From time to time, He will allow a messenger of Satan to buffet us for one reason or another. God wants to strip us of our unrighteousness and clothe us with His righteousness. He wants us to grow in the grace and knowledge of Jesus Christ, have faith in Him, and trust Him completely. He wants us to experience His miraculous power, which delivers us from Satan, the one who makes every effort to stop us from receiving blessings from God, who lives in a building not made with hands.

Many Christians allow their physical infirmities, disabilities, mental states of mind, children, loved ones, household chores, burdens, problems, and afflictions, as well as rain, snow, and even sunshine, to stop them from pressing their way to the Lord's house on Sunday. It seems they can find all kinds of excuses to stay home from church. No matter how many excuses a person comes up with, staying home will not let that individual hear the message of salvation, hope, healing, and deliverance. Jesus is not pleased with our excuses. He said in Mark 2:27 that the "Sabbath was made for man, not man for the Sabbath" (NIV).

I remember when stores were closed on Sundays and when people did household chores and cooking on Saturdays. On Sundays, we would come home from the Sunday morning worship service, heat up our dinner, eat it, and then go back to church for a Sunday afternoon worship service. For us, Sunday was a day of rest. It was the Lord's Day then, and it is still the Lord's Day now.

I have friends who are Jewish and observe the Sabbath on Saturdays. I had a conversation with a rabbi one day, and we shared our faiths and belief in God. We talked about how we observe the Lord's Day on different days. His Jewish Sabbath day is Saturday. As a Christian, my Sabbath is on Sunday. He shared with me during our conversation that someone once left the light on in a room that he had to sleep in after working overtime. He explained to me that he had to go to sleep with the light on. He could not turn the light off, because it was his Sabbath. Turning off the light was considered an act of work. The point he was making to me during this conversation was that it was the Lord's Day, and he had to observe it according to his faith and religious practices. Turning off a light might seem like a minor issue to some of us, especially when some of us personally come up with all sorts of excuses to stay home from church on the Lord's Day. However, for the rabbi, turning the light off on the Sabbath Day was a serious matter. For him, that act would have been violating the Sabbath, not honoring it. He truly believed that the "Sabbath was made for man, not man for the Sabbath."

As Christians, we need to put aside all of our excuses concerning why we can't serve the Lord on the Lord's Day. According to God's holy Word, the days of excuses are over. God deserves our worship. He deserves our praise. He deserves all honor and glory, because all honor and glory belong to Him and Him only. Every good and perfect gift comes from God. The Lord is good to each and every one of us—not some of the time, but all of the time. The sun shines on the just and unjust alike. The rain falls on you and on me. God loves us unconditionally. He gave us His only begotten Son, Jesus Christ, who died on an old, rugged cross in order to cleanse us of our sins and reconcile us back to God. The Word of God says in 2 Corinthians 5:21, "God made him who had no sin to be sin for us, so that in him we might become the righteousness of God" (NIV).

We have so much to worship God for. God pours out His grace upon all of us even though we don't deserve it. The healing Christ is always waiting for us to come to Him so that He can prove to us how much He loves us and show us He can make a way out of no way. He can make the impossible possible.

The Woman's Healing

THE DESCRIPTION OF THE WOMAN'S healing contains words of truth. Jesus called to her and said in Luke 13:12, "Woman, you are set free from your infirmity." Jesus spoke words of assurance to the woman even before she came close to Him. He laid His miraculous hands upon her, and immediately, she stood up straight. She was healed from her bent condition and stood up straight immediately before all present in the synagogue. When Jesus spoke to the woman, it was as if He said to her, "My beloved daughter, you belong to God and not to the demonic spirit of infirmity."

Jesus made this woman's soul and body whole. Jesus didn't just meet only her physical need but also her spiritual need. His act of mercy increased the woman's faith in Him. When Jesus lays His hands on us to heal us from our infirmities, He also leaves evidence of a deeper cure. In this woman's case, her bodily cure was a visible sign of an inward change in her life.

When Jesus delivered me from taking eight pills a day, consisting of antidepressants and tranquilizers, for five years, and mental illness, He healed me not only physically and mentally but also spiritually. He healed my sin-sick soul and saved me from the penalty of sin and death. Maybe you can testify about how Jesus healed you from some type of physical or mental ailment. Whatever the deliverance was, hopefully you realized that the Great Physician healed you of a bent-over condition and delivered you from the penalty of sin, death, and hell. If you can testify to this, then Jesus gave you and me a gift—the gift of eternal life. Romans 6:23 says, "For the wages of sin is death, but the gift of God is eternal life in Christ Jesus our Lord" (NIV).

If you are seeking healing from the miraculous hand of Christ, then maybe you need to ask yourself this question: Do I want to be made whole by the healing hands of the Great Physician and give Him the glory, or do I want to be cured just enough to give me a temporary rest from my sickness? I hope your answer is that you desire to be made completely whole. Too many of God's people seek temporary cures for their sicknesses. They put Band-Aids, so to speak, on whatever is wrong with them and with the things of the world. They settle for quick fixes and do not seek a permanent and eternal weight in glory. A temporary fix does not cure a person's soul, nor does it make one whole in Jesus Christ. If you are suffering from any type of illness, I encourage you to seek holistic healing from Jesus Christ. Jesus performed a miracle in the physical, mental, and spiritual realms of the bent-over woman's life, and He has the same power today to heal you. Jesus will deliver you so that you can grow spiritually, increase your faith in Him, worship Him in spirit and truth, and witness to others about His saving grace.

The Religious Ruler and the Sabbath

DURING THE COURSE OF MY life, I have encountered people from different denominations who like to argue about observing the Sabbath on Saturday instead of Sunday. They give whole dissertations on why Christians are wrong for worshipping God on the first day of the week instead of the seventh day of the week. However, they fail to realize that every born-again believer, in the name of Jesus Christ, observes Sunday, the new Christian Sabbath, as their Sabbath day. Our testimony to a dying world must always be that we celebrate the Christian Sabbath on Sunday, the first day of the week, because Jesus was resurrected from the dead early on the third day after His death. This is the Christian belief. Yet at the same time, we must give the scribes and Pharisees their due, because they knew that only through observance of their religious beliefs and laws could they preserve the purity of Israel and fulfill her mission in the world. I mention this because we must understand that over the centuries, there were always contentions between the synagogue leaders and the early church. This conflict existed even during Jesus's earthly ministry.

When Jesus was in the synagogue on the Sabbath day, when He healed the woman who had the spirit of infirmity, there was a big clash between Him and the ruler of the synagogue. The conflict concerned working on and observing the Sabbath. You and I must respect and understand that the law was something like the yoke of the Kingdom for the Jewish nation. The ruler of the synagogue not only attacked the people for any laxness in observing the Sabbath but also condemned Jesus for healing a daughter of Abraham on the Sabbath.

Luke tells of two other instances when Jesus healed on the Sabbath. In Luke 6:6–11, he talks about Jesus healing a man who had a withered hand, and in Luke 14:1–6, he speaks about the healing of a man with dropsy. Both healings occurred on the Sabbath day. Jewish tradition supported His actions, because some work was allowed on the Jewish Sabbath. Jesus said to the ruler in Luke 13:15, "You hypocrites! Doesn't each of you on the Sabbath untie his ox or donkey from the stall and lead it out to give it water?" (NIV).

The first point Jesus made was that a man was allowed to lead his ox to water even though he was not permitted to lift a bucket or carry a bucket of water on the Sabbath. In the same way, healing the woman on the Sabbath was an act of necessity. This is equivalent to a doctor who has to work on Sundays because his patients need his medical expertise. Another example of an act of necessity would be a police officer who has to work on Sundays to help keep law and order in the land. When I worked for the post office, some of my coworkers and I had to work on Sundays because we had mandated shifts, and Sunday was part of our weekly schedule. We did not have enough seniority to have Sundays off. That was our job. The mail had to be delivered the next day.

The second reason Jesus gave for what seemed to be a major violation of the law was the worth of a human life. Jesus said to the ruler of the synagogue in Luke 13:16, "Then should not this woman, a daughter of Abraham, whom Satan has kept bound for eighteen long years, be set free on the Sabbath day from what bound her?" (NIV).

The woman's life was more important to Jesus than the ox. He regarded her as the apple of His eye. Jesus was concerned about the demonic power of Satan binding her. He was concerned about setting her free by His miraculous powers. Freeing her was more important to Jesus than an ox's bondage by a rope. To Jesus, a woman living for eighteen years with a spirit of infirmity was more pitiable than an animal tied for a few hours. Therefore, Jesus was justified in His actions.

The third reason Jesus gave for what seemed like a major violation of the law on the Sabbath was a conscience issue. Jesus's conscience spoke to Him through the voice of God, His Father. He always obeyed the voice of His Father. Perhaps He heard His Father say, "Should not this woman, a daughter of Abraham, whom Satan has kept bound for eighteen long years, be set free on the Sabbath day from what bound her?" (Luke 13:16 NIV).

No mother let her sick child remain critically ill on the Lord's Day. If she had done all she could do for her child and the child's health was not improving, she would take the child to the emergency room for evaluation by a doctor. This mother would be following her conscience. She would want her child to recover from his or her illness. Medical treatment would be a work of necessity.

In light of these three reasons and these assessments, we need to ask ourselves the following questions: What does the best practice of the past teach us? What does the preciousness of human life require from each one of us? What does God command us to do by the guidance of the Holy Spirit in our lives?

It is vital for us to understand that Jesus never violated the Sabbath. He only broke the scrupulosity of the Jewish law concerning the Sabbath. You and I must be careful not to twist the Word of God around to use it as an excuse for us to work on the Sabbath and not attend church. If an act of work is not a work of necessity, then we should not do it on the Sabbath. Sunday is a day for resting and worshipping God in spirit and truth. The Sabbath is the Lord's Day and not our day. The Sabbath was made for man, not man for the Sabbath. We are to honor the Lord's Day. Just as Jesus went to the synagogue on the Sabbath to participate in the temple worship services, so must you and I participate in worship services each Sunday, our Christian Sabbath day.

Jesus embarrassed His adversaries in the controversy about the Sabbath. Because of the marvelous works Jesus performed in the synagogue, the people present rejoiced at all of the glorious things He had done.

Rejoicing in the Lord

THE TEXT IN LUKE 13 illustrates a grateful heart alive to the blessing bestowed upon it. When the woman with the spirit of infirmity immediately stood up, she praised God. Luke tells us in Luke 13:13 and 17, "Then he put his hands on her, and immediately she straightened up and praised God … The people were delighted with all the wonderful things Jesus was doing" (NIV).

When the woman came to the synagogue with her ailment, the Lord was there with His grace and mercy. She was delighted with the change she instantly experienced. Her heart rose in gratitude to the one living and true God who'd brought about a wonderful change in her life. The healed woman worshipped her healer. Jesus gave her a freedom that only He could give. She gave God the praise because He had done what no earthly physician or power could do. He'd saved her soul and made her whole. Jesus emancipated her inwardly and outwardly from the bondage that had kept her from living her life to the fullest potential physically, mentally, and spiritually. Perhaps she said to herself, *I will never be bound again with this terrible disability. My bent-over days are over. I have found my freedom in Jesus Christ. I can now walk to the synagogue while standing up straight and as a living testimony of the power of God. Therefore, I will bless the Lord at all times. His praise shall continually be in my mouth.* This act of mercy increased her faith in the One who sits on high and looks low. No wonder she glorified God. She could not keep her praise to herself. Perhaps she echoed the words of the psalmist in Psalm 146:1, 2, and 5:

> Praise the LORD. Praise the LORD, my soul.
> I will praise the LORD all my life;
> I will sing praise to my God as long as I live.
>
> Blessed are those whose help is the God of Jacob,
> whose hope is in the LORD their God. (NIV)

The people who were present in the synagogue witnessed this miracle and also glorified God. They were excited about the woman's deliverance and celebrated her marvelous healing with her. They had a sense of what was happening and judged things impartially. Those attending the synagogue experienced the humiliation of Jesus's opponents and glorified God for the things Jesus had done.

Did God ever perform a miracle in your life? If so, how did you respond to it? Did you share your testimony with other people? If you did, what were their reactions? Did they celebrate with you, or did they criticize your testimony? When God performed the miracle in your life, did you give God the glory and celebrate what He did for you?

A Glimpse of Faith and Hope

PERHAPS YOU ARE WONDERING WHAT happened to me after my radical, supernatural encounter with God. Where am I now after my deliverance thirty-eight years ago? Did I stand firm in the Lord and let nothing move me from my newfound faith in Jesus Christ? Did I turn back to my days of suffering? Or did I become more than a conqueror through Jesus Christ, who loves us? Where am I now? Well, before I let you know what has happened to me since my personal encounter with God, I would like to give you a glimpse of hope—a hope that is not deferred, because a hope deferred makes the heart sick. Rather, this hope will fill you with love, joy, and peace when you trust in Jesus Christ. Jesus promised in His Word, "All those the Father gives me will come to me, and whoever comes to me I will never drive away" (John 6:37 NIV), and "Everyone who calls on the name of the Lord will be saved" (Romans 10:13).

God also said in His Word in Isaiah 26:3, "Thou wilt keep him in perfect peace, whose mind is stayed on thee: because he trusteth in thee" (KJV).

The word *hope* has its foundation in faith. *Faith* is an action word that has tremendous power. Without faith, there is no hope. Why? Because faith treats things hoped for as a reality, no matter how impossible and hopeless things might appear to be in our lives. I would say faith and hope are twins. They see the invisible, feel the intangible, and achieve the impossible. Faith moves toward hope in the infinite God who created all things for His divine purpose and good pleasure. When we face bent-over conditions in life—such as sickness, mental illness, substance abuse, alcoholism, jealously, lying, envy, malice, hatred, physical or spiritual disabilities, and witchcraft, to name a few—Jesus invites us to come to Him. In Matthew 11:28–29, Jesus said, "Come to me, all you who are weary and burdened, and I will give you rest. Take my yoke upon you and learn from me, for I am gentle and humble in heart, and you will find rest for your souls" (NIV).

Rest Found in Jesus Alone

PRIOR TO MY RADICAL, SUPERNATURAL encounter with God, I did not have rest. I did not have the sense of security and peace that flows from a right relationship with God through His Son, Jesus Christ. I had faith and a glimpse of hope but could not find rest for my soul anywhere. Smoking cigarettes, occasionally drinking alcohol, partying, and playing cards did not give me rest. Nothing I tried during my rock-bottom days gave me rest for my soul. Furthermore, I did not have the inward peace that only Jesus can give to those who call upon His holy and righteous name.

I came to Jesus with a glimpse of faith and hope in the power of God's Word. I had no choice but to come to Him just as I was—weary, worn, sad, heavily burdened, and broken. I had to give Jesus everything I was, everything I was not, and everything I had. I placed before Him a cup of faith, filled with hope, believing Jesus would save me, heal me of my malady, and deliver me from my enemies. I believed the Master could give me unspeakable joy and the peace of God, which passes all understanding. I believed the impossible could happen to me, and it did—and it can happen to you too. How do I know? I will tell you how I know, in case you are going through a rock-bottom experience or experiencing some kind of brokenness in your life. I want to give you a glimpse of hope in God, who sits on high and looks low. Why? Because a glimpse faith and hope in Jesus Christ is all you need to be saved and delivered from your malady. I celebrate who Jesus is, because He took the little bit of faith and hope I had in Him and performed miraculous acts in my life in many ways. The Word of God tells us in Matthew 17:20, "If you have faith as small as a mustard seed, you can say to this mountain, 'Move from here to there,' and it will move. Nothing will be impossible for you" (NIV).

Maybe you feel as if your faith is not strong enough for you to go to Jesus and ask Him to deliver you or heal you. Or perhaps you think your sins are so great that Jesus will not save you. If you feel this way about your bent-over condition, I have good news for you. Matthew 17:20 talks about mustard-seed-sized faith. A mustard seed is the smallest of all seeds on Earth. If you exercise even mustard-seed-sized faith when you approach Jesus, you will be exercising enough faith and hope for Jesus Christ to save, heal, or deliver you from your bent-over condition. What matters is the quality, not the quantity, of your faith in Jesus's ability to save, heal and deliver you. As long as you are breathing, there is always hope in the saving grace of Jesus Christ. Hebrews 11:1 says, "Now *faith* is confidence in what we *hope* for and assurance about what we do not see" (NIV, emphasis mine).

Moving Forward, Upward, and Onward

SO WHERE AM I NOW? Let me testify a little bit about my journey of faith with God since He delivered me from my enemies and from taking eight pills a day, after I did so for five years. Remember, I was a legalized drug addict walking around like a zombie for five years prior to my deliverance. I existed on four Elavil, fifty milligrams each, and four Valium, ten milligrams each, every day during those five years. I was living, but I was not alive until Jesus delivered me. It is amazing what Jesus can do when you call on His name and ask Him to save you from all of your troubles and fears. The psalmist says it this way: "I call on the LORD in my distress and he answers me" (Psalm 120:1 NIV), and "I sought the LORD, and he answered me; he delivered me from all my fears" (Psalm 34:4 NIV).

I Am a Witness

REGARDING WHAT I AM ABOUT to share with you, all the glory, honor, and praise go to God for what He has done for me during my Christian journey. I cannot tell you everything, but I will share some things with you concerning what the Lord has done for me since my deliverance.

When God delivered me in October 1977 from all the medication I was taking, including nitroglycerin, I was attending a revival an evangelist held. During the revival—I remember it as clearly as if it happened yesterday—I was slain in the Spirit while praising God. I will attempt to explain to you to the best of my ability what happened to me during my radical encounter with Jesus. No matter how I describe this experience, I will never be able to do it justice. If I could show you this experience on video, I would do so, but that is not possible. The only thing I can do is try to share it with you. Perhaps you are wondering why I want to share this experience with you. I am sharing this with you because I believe that what happened to me can happen to you. I am sharing this miracle and experience with you because you might be living in a hopeless situation and looking for Christ to deliver you. I am sharing this experience with you so that you will keep hope alive when you're suffering from a bent-over condition in your life. I need to tell you that God is still saving, healing, and delivering people even today because of His unlimited love, grace, and mercy. I know this is true because He delivered me from my medication, depression, mental illness, and misery. The Word of God tells us in Ephesians 2:8–9, "For it is by grace you have been saved, through faith—and this is not from yourselves, it is the gift of God, not by works, so that no one can boast" (NIV).

Therefore, my boasting will be unto the Lord, who deserves all of the highest praise. My soul shouts hallelujah to the King of Kings and Lord of Lords.

After being slain in the Spirit, I landed on the floor. While I lay there, I felt as if I were stretched out on my own personal cross in the presence of the Lord. While lying there, the message of Luke 9:23 came to my mind:

> "If anyone would come after me, he must deny
> himself and take up his cross and follow me."
> I had to make a decision to follow Jesus—and
> I did.

Through this spiritual encounter, Jesus was letting me know that He had died for my sins, and when He arose from the grave, He rose for my justification. My stretch on the cross was a gentle stretch filled with the infinite love of God. However, Jesus's stretch was fueled by a radically aggressive and all-transforming resurrection power.

There's no way I can explain to you the depth of God's love in the natural realm. Jesus's infinite supernatural love is something you have to experience for yourself. While I was in that state, Jesus showed me His flowing blood, which He had shed for me. I cannot explain the color of His blood, because no earthly color would even come close to what I saw. All I can say to you is that I have never seen such a beautiful, soft color of red in my life. At the same time, the Lord revealed to me what looked like a gate with a few pearls on it, and I heard a sound from heaven that I could not identify. I did not know where the sound came from or where it went afterward. At that point in the revelation, all I wanted to do was stay in that position for as long as I could. Why? Because I felt as if I were having a face-to-face encounter with Jesus.

When the Lord released me from this heavenly encounter, I got up off the floor, full of God's infinite love—a love I could not articulate to anyone even if I tried. When I came out of the revelation, I was crying with a heart full of gratitude, joy, freedom, deliverance, peace, and, most of all, the love of God. I know I am being repetitious about God's love, but I will not apologize for this repetition. All I know is this: God is love. I know now what 1 John 4:19 means when it says, "We love him, because he first loved us" (KJV).

All I could say to everyone present at that service was "If only you had seen and experienced what I just saw and felt in Jesus. I felt an overpowering love—the unexplainable love of a God who loves everyone." While I was in that state of mind, Jesus wanted me to tell those present in the sanctuary that He loves us all, regardless of how many sins we have committed against Him and our fellow man. He wanted me to let everyone know that He will save those who believe in His redemptive work on Calvary's cross. Only the Holy Spirit could have given me those words. I cannot remember if anyone responded to what I said to those around me; however, it didn't matter to me at that moment. I was in another place—somewhere different from where I had been when I entered the sanctuary that night. I'd entered the sanctuary that night as a broken, destroyed, hopeless, and empty woman, but when I left the sanctuary, I left like a new creature in Jesus Christ, and I knew it. Second Corinthians 5:17 says, "Therefore, if anyone is in Christ, the *new* creation has come: The old has gone, the *new* is here!" (NIV, emphasis mine).

I promised God that if He used me for His glory, I would serve Him from that point on until I died. I owe Him everything. I cannot thank Him enough for what He has done for me. He saved my soul and made me whole. No one knows how truly thankful I am to my Lord—only God Himself knows. This was the beginning of my new journey in Jesus Christ. I was a new babe in Jesus Christ and was ready to grow in the grace and knowledge of my Lord. I was ready to tell a dying world that Jesus can save us from a deep pit of hell to the highest mountain top in Him. I wanted to shout from the mountain top that "the wages of sin is death, but the gift of God is eternal life in Christ Jesus our Lord" (Romans 6:23 NIV).

Where Am I Now?

THE QUESTION REMAINS: WHERE AM I now? With the help of the Holy Spirit, I have been serving the Lord from that day forward. By God's grace and mercy, I have been moving forward, upward, and onward in the name of Jesus Christ. My enemies had one plan for my life: to control my life and shape me into what they wanted me to be. But Jesus had another plan for me. He wanted to move me toward my destiny. He wanted to be not just my Savior but also the Lord of my life. My job was to surrender my life to Him, not to the world. During the process of deciding if I wanted Jesus to be the Lord of my life, I remembered the words in Jeremiah 29:11: "'For I know the plans I have for you,' declares the LORD, 'plans to prosper you and not to harm you, plans to give you hope and a future'" (NIV)

I also thought of the words the apostle Paul said to the church in Ephesus. He said to them—and is also saying to us now—in Ephesians 3:20–21,

> God can do anything, you know—far more than you could ever imagine or guess or request in your wildest dreams! He does it

not by pushing us around but by working within us, his Spirit deeply and gently within us. (MGS)

Therefore, after reading the words of the prophet Jeremiah and the apostle Paul, I started my new journey in Jesus Christ by studying His Word. I wanted to know Him not just in the in the power of His resurrection but also in the fellowship of His suffering. I knew I had to accept the whole package of knowing Jesus, which included trials and tribulations. As I think about it now, I realize I did not know what I was asking for when I asked for the fellowship of His suffering. Truly, I have had some days of suffering. Nevertheless, I won't complain, because my good days outweighed my bad days. When I think about suffering for the kingdom of God, I tell myself, "No cross, no crown." I recognized that I could not grow in Christ Jesus without letting go of my past life. In order for me to learn who I was in Christ, I let go and allowed Him to use me to my fullest potential for His glory. To this day, God is still revealing to me that I have more potential to use for His glory.

With the presence and power of the Holy Spirit in my life, I started moving forward, upward, and onward in Him. This vessel of clay was about to explore a spiritual journey that I did not earn on my own merit—a journey I could never have imagined. If I had not walked this journey in the power of the Holy Spirit, I would never have been able to move forward. During this journey, I have had ups and down, joys and sorrows, failures and accomplishments, trials and tribulations. Therefore, what I am about to share with you is coming from a humble and grateful heart. God's Word says in Matthew 22:12, "Whosoever shall exalt himself shall be abased; and he that shall humble himself shall be exalted."

By God's Power

GOD'S WORD IS ALWAYS TRUE. Therefore, I will not lift myself up, but I will lift up the name of Jesus so that He might be glorified through my life. He has a way of keeping us humble so that His will is fulfilled through our lives. He does this through His Word, our life experiences, and our relationship with Him under the anointing of the Holy Spirit, who lives in the heart of the believer. I know that without Him, I can do nothing, but I also know "I can do all things through Christ who gives me strength" (Philippians 4:13 NIV). I am going to share with you what God can do for a person who has been rejected, criticized, talked about, picked on, laughed at, and told she would never achieve anything in life, because I did not have what it takes. My enemies did not have the last word about my destiny. God had the last word and another plan for my life that proved to me I can do all things through Christ who strengthens me, regardless of what people said or will continue to say about me.

Advancing in the Lord

GOD HAS TAKEN ME ON an amazing journey since my experience in October 1977. I cannot write about my entire journey, because doing so would take volumes. However, I will tell you about some of my journey.

One of the main things I did then—and continue to do to this day—was have quiet time with God. During my time with God, He was preparing me for something I could never have imagined. He was calling me to be a minister of the gospel of Jesus Christ and a teacher of His Word. I had to question Him to make sure He was talking about me, the person who'd been told she did not have what it takes. I had to wait for confirmation from the Lord about this call. To my amazement, during a vacation in 1979, I had another supernatural encounter with Jesus. This revelation was awesome and powerful. I did not have to question the Lord about this ministerial calling on my life, because He made it clear in that encounter. After being prayerful and struggling with this call on my life, I accepted and acknowledged my calling to my late pastor. He told me he was not surprised, because he had been observing my Christian walk in the Lord for more than five years. Furthermore, he knew God had a calling on my life. My late pastor also knew the Holy Spirit was calling me to a teaching and preaching ministry. I thought, *Wow! Me?* A few weeks after I acknowledged my calling to the pastor, he put me in charge of the church's adult Bible study class. This was the beginning of God's plan for my life: a preaching and teaching ministry. Not long after, I became a Sunday school teacher, and I eventually became superintendent of Sunday school.

Following my teaching ministry, in 1980, I gave my initial sermon and was licensed to preach the gospel of Jesus Christ on Easter Sunday morning. Prior to my going to my late pastor to tell him about my calling, the Holy Spirit told me to go to school. I enrolled in Moody Bible Institute Correspondence School and took correspondence classes. In 1980, the Lord led me to attend the Connecticut School of Christian Religion for four years and then the Hartford Seminary Black Ministers Program for one year. My educational journey did not stop there. Under the inspiration of the Holy Spirit, I also attended New Hampshire College School of Human Services, where I earned my bachelor of science degree. I continued on to earn a master of arts degree in lay ministries from the Hartford Seminary. In the midst of all my schooling, I earned a bachelor of theology degree and a doctor of divinity degree from Springfield Bible Seminary. No one but God could use someone whom people had said would never achieve anything in life and did not have what it took. Only God could prove people wrong. I am amazed and thankful to

God for what He has done in the area of my education. All I had to do was surrender to His holy and righteous will. Again, only God could help me achieve these things. The apostle Paul says in Romans 12:1, "I beseech you therefore, brethren, by the mercies of God, that ye present your bodies a living sacrifice, holy, acceptable unto God, which is your reasonable service" (NIV).

The Issue of Sexism

DURING MY JOURNEY IN PURSING my education, God opened many other doors for me. After God called me into ministry, the Holy Spirit started building me up to become a leader. I soon realized God was using me as a pioneer for women in ministry. Being a woman in ministry in 1980 came with a price because of the issue of sexism. At that time, few male pastors, ministers, and leaders favorably accepted women into the Christian ministry. This rejection of women in ministry meant a female minister had to work extra hard to prove herself in ministry. I knew God had called me just as He called men into the ministry. Therefore, I could not give up. My motto was "If anyone has a problem with me as a woman in ministry, it is his or her problem." I was not going to own someone else's problem. The Word of God tells us in Galatians 3:28, "There is neither Jew nor Gentile, neither slave nor free, nor is there male and female, for you are all one in Christ Jesus" (NIV).

I was not looking to be a leader or pioneer for anyone. This was God's choice. I was too busy working hard to combat the sexism I was experiencing. I knew only that God had called me, and I did not want to disappoint Him.

During my journey, the Holy Spirit led me to join many organizations. Some of them embraced women in ministry, and some had issues with women in ministry. Most of the organizations were led by men. At that time, female ministers did not hold significant offices in some of the organizations. I did not remove my membership in these organizations because of women's rejection in ministry. I pursued the work that the Holy Spirit called me to do as a member of these organizations. By His grace, God allowed me to win the favor of some of the leaders and pastors, including some who had been against female ministers. To my amazement, the Lord raised me up to be a change agent in a couple of the organizations I belonged to.

In one case, I became the first female president of a predominantly male organization after five decades of its existence. In another instance, I became the first female pastor voted into an organization in almost a hundred years. Only years later did I recognize that God was using me to open doors for women who had been called into ministry. Additionally, my acceptance affirmed all women's, not just clergywomen's, senses of value and importance. This road was like the proverbial road less traveled; at times, it was a rough road on which to travel. Without the help of the Holy Spirit, and the amount of suffering I encountered, I would have failed miserably in this walk. God's grace sustained me during this part of my journey. People were not aware that I encountered demoralizing and debilitating sexism as a female minister. Throughout this journey, the Spirit of God kept a smile on my face and poured out His favor on me. To God be the glory—I endured by God's grace. The Word of God tells us in 1 Corinthians 15:58, "Be ye stedfast, unmoveable, always abounding in the work of the Lord, forasmuch as ye know that your labour is not in vain in the Lord" (KJV).

Entering ministry was a challenge because as a woman, I was still trying to find out where I fit in an arena controlled predominantly by men. Sexism was a big struggle and a test for me. I faced many obstacles because I was a woman. But by the grace of God, I let none of these things move me. I knew who I was and whose I was. I was God's child. He promised He would fight my battles for me in Isaiah 49:25: "I will contend with those who contend with you" (NIV).

A Continuous Journey in the Lord

IN 1993, GOD CALLED ME to start New Canaan Baptist Church, which is now the Living Word Worship Center. In the year 2000, the Holy Spirit led me to start an outreach ministry called Pastoral Resource Ministries. This ministry's mission is to improve people's quality of life through a holistic approach, by providing education, counseling, and other programs and supportive services. The Holy Spirit continued opening doors for me, and I've served on the boards of directors for faith-based and community-based organizations, including the Mayor's Alcohol and Drug Intervention Coalition for the City of Hartford. Over the course of my thirty-five years in ministry, the Lord has blessed me to receive many service awards from religious and secular communities. By the grace of God, I have been blessed to minister throughout the United States.

Why am I saying all of this to you? God took this broken vessel—a person who was a victim of witchcraft, addicted to eight pills a day, and shattered into a million pieces—and put her back together again. I am glad I was not like Humpty Dumpty, who had a great fall. Nobody could put him back together again. But praise be to God that you and I are precious children of God. He can fix your brokenness, just as He fixed my brokenness. He is still repairing me to this day in many areas of my life. I am saying this to you in case you are living with a sense of hopelessness and despair. There is always hope in our Lord and Savior, Jesus Christ. He can put your broken pieces back together again in ways you could never imagine. Jesus is still performing miracles today. In Luke 13:13, the Word of God tells us what happened after Jesus put His hands on a daughter of Abraham unable to stand upright. She "immediately straightened up" and "praised God." I cannot tell you if she shouted, ran around the synagogue, cried, smiled, waddled on the floor, or ran out of the synagogue to tell people in the street what Jesus had done for her, but I can tell you that as I write these words and reflect on that day in October 1977, tears of joy are streaming down my face for the miraculous things God has done for me in my past, is doing for me in my present, and will do for me in my future. As I reflect on that day, my entire being praises God for the miracles in my life.

The lyrics of Carl Ferdinand Wilhelm's hymn "Wholehearted Thanksgiving to Thee I Will Bring," with music by W. Howard Doane, and the first two lines of Fanny Crosby's refrain to "God Be the Glory" express how I feel about God and all the blessings He has bestowed upon me.

Wholehearted thanksgiving to Thee I will bring;
In praise of Thy marvelous works I will sing,
In Thee I will joy and exultingly cry Thy Name

I will praise, O Jehovah Most High.

Praise the Lord, praise the Lord, let the earth hear His voice!
Praise the Lord, praise the Lord, let the people rejoice!
O come to Jehovah, declare ye His fame,
And give Him all honor, for just is His Name.[38]

To God be the glory!

---

[38] *The Cyber Hymnal*, accessed September 26, 2015, http://www.hymntime.com/tch/htm/w/h/t/wht2tiwb.htm.

Bibliography

Bancroft, D. D. *Elemental Theology, Doctrinal and Conservative.* Hayward, California: J. F. May Press, 1948.

Bible Hub. Last modified 2014. http://www.biblehub.com/niv/matthew/6-5.htm.

Copeland, Germaine. "Too Busy to Pray." March 2003. http://www.prayers.org/articles/article_mar03.asp.

The Free Dictionary. s. vv. "judgmental," "criticism," "faultfinding." Last modified 2015. http://www.thefreedictionary.com

Haley, H. H. *Haley Bible Handbook.* Grand Rapids, Michigan: Zondervan, 1965.

Lockyer, Herbert. *All the Miracles of the Bible.* Grand Rapids, Michigan: Zondervan, 1961.

Merriam Webster's Collegiate Dictionary. 10th ed. Springfield, Massachusetts: Merriam Webster Inc., 2002.

Miller, Madeleine S., and J. Lane. *The New Harper's Bible Dictionary.* New York: Harper and Row, 1890.

—————. *Synagogues and Rulers*. New York: Harper and Row, 1973.

Nelson's Illustrated Bible Dictionary. Nashville: Thomas Nelson, 1986.

Osbeck, Kenneth W. *101 Hymn Stories*. Grand Rapids, Michigan: Kregel Publications, 2012.

"The Brown Scapular." Last modified 2011. http://www.overcomeproblems.com/miracles.htm.

Author's Profile

THE REVEREND DR. THELMA GILBERT was ordained into the gospel ministry of Jesus Christ in 1986. She is recognized as a competent, qualified, and well-trained teacher, leader, pastor, and servant. Well prepared, disciplined, cheerful, and confident, Thelma serves as an advocate for people of all ages who are oppressed, suffering, and heartbroken from the many ills of our society. Dr. Gilbert's God-given gifts, talents, and services as an acclaimed teacher, seminar speaker, and preacher are sought across the United States.

She received her bachelor of theology degree from Springfield Christian Bible Seminary Association in Springfield, Massachusetts, and a bachelor of science degree in human services from New Hampshire College in Manchester, New Hampshire. She earned a master of arts degree in lay ministries from Hartford Seminary in Hartford, Connecticut, and a doctor of divinity degree from Springfield Christian Bible Seminary Association in Springfield, Massachusetts.

Thelma currently works as a community support specialist for the Village in Hartford, Connecticut. She is a former employee of the University of Connecticut School of Social Work, where she held the position of organizational skills and development consultant and project manager.

Dr. Gilbert is the chief executive officer and founder of Pastoral Resource Ministries Inc. (PRM) and Pastor of The Living Word Worship Center (TLWWC), both of Bloomfield, Connecticut.

Dr. Gilbert is a pioneer and mentor for women in ministry. In 1987, at the fifty-seventh annual Session of the Interdenominational Ministerial Alliance of Greater Hartford, Connecticut, she was voted the organization's first female president. In 1996, at the ninety-second annual Session of the Connecticut State Missionary Baptist Convention, she became the first female pastor voted into full membership of that organization. She was the recipient of the Humanitarian Award from the Greater Hartford Club of the National Association of Negro Business and Professional Women's Club Inc. in 1997, the Significant Ministry Award from Hartford Seminary in 2000, the Lifetime Achievement Award from the Sons of Thunder Coalition in 2003, and the Martin Luther King Drum Major Award from the Interdenominational Ministerial Alliance of Greater Hartford in 2011.

Thelma resides in Bloomfield, Connecticut. She is the mother of two children and the grandmother of seven grandchildren.

One of her favorite Scriptures is Proverbs 3:5–6: "Trust in the Lord with all your heart and lean not on your own understanding; in all your ways acknowledge him, and he will make your paths straight."

Printed in the United States
By Bookmasters